How to get a
DIVORCE IN MARYLAND

First Edition

By Richard S. Granat

The Washington Book Trading Company
Arlington, Virginia

Disclaimer
This book is designed to provide accurate and authoritative information with respect to the subject matter covered. It is sold with the understanding that neither the publisher nor the author is engaged in rendering legal or other professional services. If legal advice or other expert assistance is required, the services of a competent attorney or other professional person should be sought. While every attempt is made to provide accurate information, the author or the publisher cannot be held accountable for errors or omissions.

First Edition
Copyright 1998 by Richard S. Granat
All rights reserved
I.S.B.N. Number 0-915168-48-0 $24.95

Published by The Washington Book Trading Company
P.O. Box 1676, Arlington VA 22210 (703) 525-6873
Raissa M. Modrak, Books Editor
Type by Gerryamanda, Washington DC
Printed by Balmar Printing, Gaithersburg MD

Dedication
To my wife, Nancy, for her support and for bearing with me
during this project.

About the Author
Richard S. Granat, J.D.,
is a member of the District of Columbia Bar and the Maryland Bar and
has been a Clinical Supervisor to the Assisted Domestic Relations *Pro Se*
Project at the University of Maryland School of Law and Director of The
People's Law Library of Maryland, an on-line legal resource for Maryland's citizens at http://www.peoples-law.com on the World Wide Web. He
also maintains an on-line law practice located at http://www.granat.com
that is limited to family law and also sponsors the Divorce Law Information Center at http://www.divorcelawinfo.com on the World Wide Web.

Acknowledgments
To Nathalie Gilfrich, J.D., the first Project Director for the Assisted
Domestic Relations *Pro Se* Project at the University of Maryland Law
School, for writing the section on custody and visitation, developing the
step-by-step instructions, general editorial assistance, and practical
suggestions.

To Michael Millemann, Director, Clinical Director, University of Maryland
School of Law, who had the courage to start a legal assistance program for
pro se litigants in family matters within a traditional law school.

To Jo B. Fogel, J.D., of Rockville, Maryland, for reviewing the law
portions of this book. It is a pleasure to thank her for comments,
suggestions, knowledge of Maryland law, and especially her dedication
as a family law practitioner.

To Sandra Kalenik, writer, for her pioneering work in this field.

Preface

This is the first edition of **How to Get a Divorce in Maryland**. It is the lineal descendent of the five editions of *How To Get A Divorce in the District of Columbia, Maryland, and Virginia*, originally authored by Sandra Kalenik in 1976, and subsequently revised and edited by myself in 1989. This book, unlike the first, concentrates only on Maryland law, and contains forms and instructions for not only obtaining a divorce action, but also custody and visitation actions; child support, child support collection, and child support modification actions (a revised edition for Virginia and the District of Columbia is scheduled to follow). The need for this expanded version is caused by the approval and release by the Maryland court system of a set of simplified *pro se* legal forms that make it much easier for parties to represent themselves in a domestic relations action in Maryland. A copy of these forms, with instructions on how to use them, are contained in this book. Since 1994, when the fifth edition of the earlier book was published, the number of individuals representing themselves in domestic actions in Maryland courts has increased dramatically. An evaluation study conducted by the University of Maryland School of Law revealed that with the correct information, people are able to represent themselves in a wide range of family law cases successfully; that they were satisfied with the process; and that 80% would do so again if necessary. (A complete version of the study is published on the internet at: http://www.pro-selaw.org.) This book is designed to provide the information that *pro se* parties need to represent themselves effectively in domestic relations actions in Maryland.

For almost all people divorce is a wrenching, emotional experience. To make it even more difficult, the law is very much involved in every facet of divorce and its aftermath. If you are like the majority of people who obtain a divorce, then you have never had any personal experience with the law, and may easily become overwhelmed by the legal process. You have to follow definitive rules and requirements that you may not know about. You may also have rights of which you are unaware, such as your right to receive a share of your spouse's pension, your right to ask the custodial spouse not to move within a specific number of miles from your present home, and, for women, your right to have your former name restored. Knowing these rights can help you to smooth the path not only to your divorce but also to your future.

A divorce action can be a very emotional experience and is at the top of the list of stressful experiences. If I were to offer advice, it would be this: stay as calm and unemotional as you possibly can. Learn what your rights are, decide what you need and want, and keep as cool as possible. When you are feeling depressed, overwhelmed, revengeful or furious, talk it over with a friend or therapist, or take up a sport, exercise, go on a trip, or lose yourself in books. Whatever you do, try not to act out your emotions by making them a legal battlefield among you, your spouse, and any children you might have. If you have children, you want your assets devoted to them, and not spent on legal fees. If you want to argue over everything, you will spend a fortune in legal fees, and the end result is not likely to be any better than if you had sat down with your spouse as rational adults and liquidated your "partnership" in an equitable and fair manner. Often this is too much to ask of two individuals who are caught in the emotions of the moment, but if you can be detached you will save more in the long run in money, emotional energy, and the time it takes to get on with your life.

I hope this book serves you well. Please don't hesitate to send me your comments and suggestions for future editions. They will be appreciated.

Richard S. Granat. Esq.
e-mail: Richard@Granat.com
www.divorcelawinfo.com

HOW TO GET A
DIVORCE IN MARYLAND

Introduction and How to Use This Book

This book will show you not only how to do your divorce in the State of Maryland, but also how to represent yourself in uncontested child custody and visitation actions and child support and child support modification actions. This book contains all of the forms and information you need to handle these actions on your own, without incurring the expense of legal fees. Although you can use these forms for contested actions, it is not advisable. If you can resolve your dispute with your spouse outside of the court system, your case becomes "uncontested" and then processing your legal documents through the court system is relatively straightforward. In almost all cases, if you have the correct legal information you will not have to hire an attorney. This book is designed to provide you with this information.

This book is not meant to replace the advice of an attorney. You may need some legal advice in order to fully understand the rights and obligations of each spouse. You can save on legal fees if you purchase this legal advice only, and make your divorce and other family issues a matter of agreement rather than conflict. Couples who can communicate openly and resolve issues between themselves can reach their own agreement and dissolve their marriage with a minimum of lawyer involvement. Both sides must be willing to compromise, but it is worth taking the trouble to resolve all the issues in a separation or property settlement agreement, which becomes final once the divorce decree is issued.

This book will enable Marylanders who are going through a divorce to:
* learn about the entire process, including how to select an attorney if needed;
* become informed decision-makers about issues such as child custody and visitation, child support, and marital property division;
* understand the function and the elements of a Marital Separation Agreement;
* learn about mediation as a method of resolving domestic conflicts;
* prepare the legal forms for divorce, child support, child custody, and visitation actions;
* and learn how to file these documents and get a legal result.

This book will help you represent yourself in routine, uncontested matters. You will need the assistance of an attorney if:
* your spouse is already represented by an attorney and has filed for divorce;
* your spouse has filed for divorce and you want to contest it;
* you and your spouse cannot come to an agreement on key issues, in which case you need to try mediation first;
* you have complex assets such as a holding in a private company, a pension, or extensive real estate which requires evaluation before an agreement on dividing property can be drafted;
* or you think that your spouse is hiding assets, not dealing with you in good faith, or has a history of domestic violence.
In all of these situations you should seriously think about retaining an attorney to represent you.

Part 1 of this book provides an overview of the divorce process in Maryland, including discussions of child custody and visitation, child support, marital property issues, and sample Marital Separation Agreements that will help you with your divorce or domestic relations action. At the end of this section you will find a glossary of legal terms, addresses and phone numbers of Maryland courts.

Part 2 provides general instructions and step-by-step instructions along with a set of the Maryland Domestic Relations *Pro Se* Forms that you can copy and use to file your actions.

HOW TO GET A
DIVORCE IN MARYLAND

Contents *i*
Introduction and How to Use This Book *vii*

Part 1

Part 2

Do You Need A Lawyer?

No matter how civil relations are between spouses, one spouse has to charge the other spouse in a court or court-like proceeding in order to get a divorce, even if the divorce is non-contested. Regardless of how private you are or would like to be about your personal problems, you must spell out the facts to a judge or a judicial intermediary in order to obtain a divorce. Your goal is to get a judgment.

Your Divorce and the Legal System

There are two routes to getting a judgment. The most common course is to hire a lawyer, tell him or her the facts, and hope for the best. When one party retains a lawyer, the other is almost compelled to also retain an attorney. Once both parties retain lawyers they become enmeshed in the adversarial legal system to get their judgment. Now both parties must communicate through their attorneys. Every step becomes a step in an adversarial process. It costs money, time, and aggravation because the court system is not the best institution to decide the custody of your children, or what visitation times should be allowed, how you divide your property, and who should be allowed to remain in the family home. Empowering the courts to decide these issues means that lawyers are with you every step of the way. Divorce then becomes a very expensive process.

Once you go down the adversarial path you lose control over your dispute—the lawyers own your dispute, not you.

Divorce is never an easy process, but you can minimize the expense, the emotional cost and stress, and the time it takes by understanding how you can avoid going through the adversarial system. The secret is to know how to go around the legal system by reaching an agreement with your spouse without first going to court and making your divorce uncontested. By reaching agreement yourselves, you have far more control over your dispute and can work out far better solutions. Research on the outcome of divorce supports the idea that active participation in managing your divorce leads to better outcomes. A good outcome or result means that there is less post-divorce conflict, agreements are adhered to, there is more good will, and the relationships between both parents and the children are better. This doesn't mean that you do not get advice or help from an attorney or mediator—it simply means that you should know the rules and be in charge of managing your case. It is also much cheaper than full representation by an attorney.

Divorce the Easy Way

Uncontested vs. Contested Divorce and Other Family Matters

A divorce or other family legal action is uncontested if both you and your spouse want a divorce and both of you agree about the following: (1) who will have custody of the children; (2) how much the parent who does not have custody of the children will contribute toward their support; (3) who will be responsible for any debts you may have; and (4) how you will divide up your property and belongings, such as a house, any furniture, bank accounts, pensions, and other assets.

If you and your spouse disagree about any of these issues, the divorce is contested. In a contested divorce, you will probably need to be represented by an attorney.

Other family legal matters can be contested or uncontested. Suppose for example, there is an outstanding child support order, and the parent paying child support becomes unemployed. If there is a change of 25% in that parent's income, the child support can be modified. If both parents agree there should be a change in the child support, they can enter into a stipulation to change the order, and the matter is uncontested. If for some reason the custodial parent opposes the change, the matter becomes contested.

Or suppose, there is an outstanding visitation order and both parents agree that the visitation schedule should be changed. If both agree and file an agreement to amend the visitation schedule (called a "stipulation"), the matter is uncontested. If they want to fight about it in a court hearing, the matter is contested.

Entering Into a Marital Settlement Agreement

The key to maintaining control over your conflict is not to retain an attorney and to reach agreement with your spouse, preferably by entering into a Marital Settlement Agreement, at the time you separate and before your divorce gets underway.

A Marital Settlement Agreement becomes part of the Judgment for your divorce and controls all the behavior of the parties both during the period of separation and after the divorce decree is granted. The Marital Settlement Agreement enables you to control all the terms of agreement between you and your spouse.

With a good Marital Settlement Agreement in hand, the rest of the divorce process is simply paperwork and managing your way through the red tape of the court system. While this may take some time, it is much less costly than the traditional way—in which both parties are represented by attorneys who negotiate with each other, often up to the day before a trial is scheduled to begin, in order to reach the same Marital Settlement Agreement that the parties could have arrived at if they had been reasonable with each other. However, by this time you and your spouse are financially and emotionally exhausted.

Avoiding a High-Conflict Divorce

The key to an "easy" divorce with minimum conflict is to never "retain" an attorney, unless you fit into one or more of the major exceptions to this rule that are discussed in this section.

This doesn't mean that you should *not* get legal assistance or legal advice if you think you need it. The critical word is "retain," which means hiring an attorney to represent you in every aspect of your case. Once you sign a "retainer agreement" and pay a $1,000–$10,000 retainer fee, your lawyer has taken control of your case. And they literally take over your case and bring it into the high-conflict court system. Indeed, professional ethics require attorneys to aggressively pursue every "right" they think you have in order to protect themselves from future malpractice claims from you as the client. Often that means quick court action and switching into an adversarial mode. Lawyers are taught in law school to be litigators, not mediators or negotiators. Yet a confrontational style is often inappropriate in a setting seeking to resolve long-term personal and family problems, particularly when children are involved.

In fact, you may need only limited legal assistance, such as a review of your Marital Settlement Agreement before you sign it, or assistance in drafting one or two clauses. By learning how to manage the relationship with your attorney, you can limit the amount of legal fees you pay and maintain control over the management of your case.

It pays to be a wise consumer of legal services. The cost of a divorce easily can equal the price of a new car, yet we are much less careful and less informed when buying legal services than when buying a new automobile. Of course, there is much more evaluative information about cars available, than there is about the quality and competence of attorneys. This is all the more reason to be very careful when purchasing professional services. Unfortunately there is no consumer report that provides reliable information about a particular attorney's performance, ethics, or credentials.

Nevertheless, there are times when you have no choice but to hire an attorney.

When a Lawyer Is Absolutely Necessary

If you have considerable personal property, children, a home, if you are a woman and have not been working, or if you and your spouse are having difficulty deciding who gets what and how much money should be given for child support and alimony, then your best—perhaps only—recourse is to see an attorney.

If your spouse is a potential danger to you; you think your spouse is hiding or transferring assets; your spouse is very hostile and/or abusive or violent; or if your spouse has cut off all sources of support and you have no place to live—then you need to be represented by an attorney. In these cases you should seek legal representation immediately.

An attorney is, or should be, very familiar with the laws of domestic relations, which govern divorce and other domestic actions. But more than that, an attorney can offer you the objective treatment your case might need, particularly if you and your spouse are arguing over everything from cars to toothpicks. A lawyer can advise you of things that you not only don't think about, but also probably don't even know about.

Most people don't think about lawyers until they are in trouble and need one. Then there is often a panic stage—what do I do, where do I go, where can I find one, whom should I get—accompanied by a lot of phone calls to friends and family, or even by a quick run through of the yellow pages.

Selecting an Attorney

It is extremely important that you choose a competent, interested attorney: one with whom you feel comfortable and who returns your phone calls, answers your questions directly, and is not always "too busy."

4 DIVORCE IN MARYLAND

In choosing a lawyer, your best bet is to ask divorced friends whom they recommend and why. Ask your friends what kind of work their lawyer has done for them, how much time the lawyer invested in the case, the outcome, and how much they were charged. Or ask an attorney to recommend someone if she doesn't do divorce work. Then, interview the attorneys.

Keep in mind that you and your lawyer will be working together as a team. It's important to find someone with whom you feel comfortable. The more you know what you want, the easier it will be to find the one you want. Be sure to ask about charges and billing. Finally, keep in mind that your attorney works for you.

Tips on Finding the Right Lawyer

Here are some tips on finding an attorney who will serve you well:

Only Hire a Lawyer With Expertise in Family Law. A lawyer who normally handles personal injury law or corporate matters won't be of much use in a divorce since he may have little better understanding of family law than you do. Maryland does not allow attorneys to state that they specialize in a particular legal field, and thus no specialty designations for attorneys exist in the State. However, firms are permitted to state that they limit their practice to family law, which means that they don't practice in other areas of the law. Another indication that a law firm has expertise in family law is if the firm is known to take on *pro bono* cases in family law. A *pro bono* case is one that the firm takes on for no fee, or a reduced fee, because the client is financially eligible for such assistance under criteria established by a local bar association or the Maryland State Bar Association. You can also ask what percentage of the lawyer's practice is devoted to domestic law cases.

Always Have a Written Agreement. Do not hire a lawyer based on an oral agreement. That only leads to misunderstandings. Instead, be sure the fee agreement (called a retainer agreement) is in writing and that you understand all of its terms.

Family Lawyers Usually Charge "By the Hour." You are going to have to keep a sharp eye on the bill. Thus, do not accept a bill that reads, "fees for services rendered." Rather, insist on a detailed monthly billing statement. If you find a mistake or there is a charge you don't understand, bring it to the attention of your lawyer. Some lawyers are experimenting with a new form of practice called *"unbundled"* legal services.

These lawyers will charge you just for the advice that you need, usually on an hourly basis, to support you in your mediation and after as a *pro se* litigant. In this case, you will still file your own legal papers, but the lawyer will be available to provide you with legal advice if you need it. You might also consider retaining an attorney to be your *pro se* coach. This means that you would be on record as representing yourself and would do the actual work on your case. The attorney would be paid an hourly fee to review your work or to help you before a hearing.

Don't Be Passive. Keep in mind that your attorney works for you. Just because you have a lawyer doesn't mean you do not have a job to do. You (not your lawyer) should make the ultimate decisions about how to proceed with your case. After all, it is your life and your future that is at stake, not your lawyer's. It is very important that you communicate to your attorney your intention to be helpful and your desire to control the decisions in your case. When the attorney–client relationship works well, you and your lawyer are partners working for a common objective—with you as the senior partner in control of the divorce.

Ask About Whatever You Don't Understand or Think You May Not Understand. Listen to what the lawyer says. Part of her job is to educate you about what you will be going through. (You may want to take notes for future reference.) Remember that you have the right to answers. Never accept a condescending answer such as, "It's too complicated, you wouldn't understand." And especially do not accept, "Trust me, it's all under control."

Some Questions to Ask Your Lawyer

Here are some sample questions you will want to ask your lawyer. You may also want to add more of your own.

➤ How long will the whole thing take?

➤ What will be happening step-by-step?

➤ What is your best estimate of the fees I will be charged?

➤ How much will the costs be? (Costs are all "out-of-pocket" expenses that are incurred to support the litigation. Examples are court filing fees and paying court reporters for deposition transcription services. Costs can mount into the thousands of dollars in contested cases.)

➤ Will I be asked to pay the other side's attorney fees? Can I have my spouse pay my attorney fees?

➤ After describing what you want out of the divorce (i.e. by way of property division, custody and support), ask: Can this be done? If not, why not? If so, what are the problems we face in getting what I want?

➤ How much support should I ask for (or offer to pay)?

➤ How can I be sure that I get my visitation, child support, alimony, etc.?

Who Pays Lawyer Fees?

Attorney's fees can be expensive, especially if your divorce is contested. Usually, your lawyer will require a retainer fee, ranging from a low of $500 to a high of $15,000. Hourly rates range from a low of $90 for recent law school graduates to $250–$300 an hour for lawyers who have built metropolitan-wide reputations in the divorce field. The retainer is based on whether the case is contested or uncontested, the amount of property involved, how much time will be involved, what issues are in dispute, and whether there is a custody battle or a fight over the amount of child support payments or alimony. In a hotly contested divorce case, fees could run as high as $10,000–$100,000.

Deciding who pays those legal fees could be a battle in itself—and often is. Each person could pay for his or her own attorney, the husband could be required to pay all fees, or the party at fault in a contested case could be ordered to pay. Basically, this is another issue that should be negotiated by your attorney.

Taxes and Lawyer Fees

There is some small tax relief when it comes to your legal fees: all of the time spent conversing with your lawyer that relates directly to taxes is deductible from your income taxes. If your lawyer charges $200 an hour and you spend three hours talking about your taxes and future tax status, you can deduct $600.

Help With Finding a Lawyer

You might consider going to the following places to find an attorney to help you with your divorce or other family law matter. Check your phone directory or information for current phone numbers.

Family Law Hotline, Women's Law Center, 1-800-845-8550
Lawyer Referral Service, Montgomery County Bar Association
Lawyer Referral Service, Bar Association of Baltimore City
Legal Assistance of Prince George's County
Legal Aid Bureau, Baltimore City and State-Wide
People's Pro Bono Action Center, Inc.
Maryland Volunteers Lawyers Service

If You Think You Qualify for Legal Aid

The Maryland Legal Aid Bureau is the state-wide legal services organization providing legal assistance in civil matters to low income individuals and families. Unfortunately because of recent cutbacks in Federal funds and new restrictions on how those funds should be spent, the Legal Aid Bureau doesn't handle the run-of-the-mill divorce case. You may be able to get assistance if you have a hotly contested custody case and there is evidence of domestic abuse. Despite the high volume of domestic cases in the Maryland court system, Maryland's Legal Aid Bureau assigns them a low priority. Your best alternative, if you can't afford an attorney, is to seek an assignment of a private attorney through one of the bar association *pro bono* programs or to represent yourself using the *pro se* forms in this book.

Referral Services

Most bar association referral services will charge you an initial fee of approximately $20–$35 to refer you for a half-hour consultation with an attorney. After that, the fee is between you and the attorney, who may charge you a flat rate, or by the hour. Beware of these bar association referral services. Not only do they charge you a fee (they should be free with the attorney picking up the cost of the referral), but also they assign lawyers to clients based on a sequential list. There is no correlation between the lawyer's expertise in family law and your need for someone with such an expertise. As discussed above, bar rules in Maryland prohibit attorneys from representing that they specialize in a particular substantive area. This assumes that all attorneys have equal competence in all substantive areas. Of course this is absurd. If you have a brain tumor you consult with a neurosurgeon, not a general practitioner. On the other hand, if you only need an aspirin you go to a pharmacist, not an internist. The analogy is that if you have a non-contested matter and only have to file routine legal documents and you have the correct information on how to do it, you do not need the skills of an experienced trial lawyer.

You might find the skills of an experienced paralegal helpful, but unfortunately, as in most of the United States, and unlike almost every other country in the world, in Maryland paralegals and other non-lawyers are not permitted to offer limited legal services to the public.

Doing It Yourself

You can save on legal fees if your divorce or family law matter is uncontested and by doing the work involved with composing the marital agreement yourselves and filing your own legal pleadings. Many people handle routine family law matters without retaining an attorney. In California, 70% of all uncontested divorces are completed by unrepresented *pro se* litigants. Family mediation is also a process that is often handled by the parties without representation by counsel. Each party's attorney should review a draft of the Marital Settlement Agreement before it is executed. It may be that certain key issues have been overlooked or that some procedures have changed since the publication of this book. If you have a pension or a large amount of property or income, it is certainly advisable to consult an attorney before you sign a final agreement. An attorney can also be very helpful in advising you during the mediation itself. You can save substantial legal fees in routine matters by finding an attorney who will provide you with discrete services when you need it, and then handling the rest of the paperwork yourself using the forms and instructions in this book.

How You Can Save on Legal Fees

In 1995, the Circuit Courts in Maryland approved and released a set of domestic relations forms specifically designed for *pro se* filers. *Pro se* is the Latin term for someone who represents himself/herself in court without an attorney. *Pro se* means "for one's self." Once a marital property settlement agreement is reached, you can file all of your court documents yourself without the assistance of an attorney. The actual completion and filing of these legal documents, and preparing yourself for a hearing, is routine, and you can save significant amounts of money by completing your own forms and doing the filing yourself, rather than using an attorney's services.

Filing Your Own Legal Documents as a Pro Se Party

Representing oneself in court is a time-honored tradition in American jurisprudence that has recently become even more widespread as legal fees have soared and legal information has become more accessible. You have an absolute right to represent yourself in court in Maryland. In addition to reducing or eliminating the cost of legal fees, you will have personal control in a legal procedure that affects your life. Too often, a feeling of powerlessness within a marriage is made worse by the process of getting divorced. In a *pro se* divorce or legal proceeding, you will be asserting control over your own life by personally managing the change in your marriage status. Finally, whenever people represent themselves in court proceedings, it shows other people that they also can represent themselves, and that the court

Filing Pro Se

system is something to which all of us can and should have access.

Doing It Yourself

Doing it yourself is not encouraged by the court, but that doesn't mean you should not do it. If you want to keep the financial cost to a minimum, and there are no major contested issues, it is the only way to go. The staff at the courthouse are generally courteous and desire to be helpful, but they are not attorneys and are not permitted to give legal advice. They can't tell a person how to comply with the legal requirements of filing papers with the court. They usually can provide assistance by showing you a sample of prior pleadings that have been accepted by the court, and they will explain what pleadings must be filed, what fees must be paid and how to get a hearing scheduled. The rest of the information you need is contained in this book.

The Domestic Relations Pro Se Forms

These new domestic relations *pro se* forms (now called the Dom. Rel. forms) make it much easier to complete your legal pleadings without retaining an attorney to complete your paper work. A complete set of the Dom. Rel. forms appears in Part 2 of this book. They are available to the public at the Clerk's office of the Circuit Court in every county in Maryland. You can also retrieve a copy of the forms at several locations on the World Wide Web on the internet: at http://www.divorcelawinfo.com and http://www.maritalstatus.com, for example.

You can even complete these forms on-line and print them out on your local printer at The People's Law Library of Maryland on the World Wide Web at http://www.peoples-law.com.

The forms deal with: Divorce (Limited and Absolute); Custody and Visitation (Complaints, Modifications, and Contempt); and Child Support (Complaints, Modifications, and Contempt). Here is a complete list.

Child Support, Custody, and Visitation Forms
Dom. Rel. 1, Complaint for Child Support
Dom. Rel. 2, Petition for Contempt (Failure to Pay Child Support)
Dom. Rel. 3, Petition for Contempt (Denial of Visitation)
Dom. Rel. 4, Complaint for Custody
Dom. Rel. 5, Complaint for Visitation
Dom. Rel. 6, Petition/Motion to Modify Child Support
Dom. Rel. 7, Petition/Motion to Modify Custody/Visitation
Divorce Forms
Dom. Rel. 20, Complaint for Absolute Divorce
Dom. Rel. 21, Complaint for Limited Divorce
Financial Forms
Dom. Rel. 30, Financial Statement (Child Support)
Dom. Rel. 31, Financial Statement (Alimony or Child Support)
Dom. Rel. 32, Motion for Waiver of Pre-Payment of Filing Fees
      and Other Court Costs
Dom. Rel. 33, Joint Statement of Parties Concerning Marital and
      Non-Marital Property
Other Forms
Dom. Rel. 50, Answer to Complaint/Petition/Motion
Dom. Rel. 51, Request for Master's Hearing
Dom. Rel. 52, Request for Trial on the Merits

Dom. Rel. 53, Show Cause Order
Dom. Rel. 54, Request for Order of Default
Dom. Rel. 55, Affidavit of Service (Private Process)
Dom. Rel. 56, Affidavit of Service (Certified Mail)
Dom. Rel. 57, Order

Who Should Not Use the Domestic Relations Forms?

If you have a case that truly requires the expertise of a lawyer, either because of the necessity to know the rules of evidence or the subtleties of the law that has to be argued, you should not use the Dom. Rel. forms or file as a *pro se* litigant. Some examples of these types of cases include: contested custody, divorces involving substantial property and/or pension issues, and child support cases where you want to pay less than the guidelines require. Additionally, if an attorney represents the other party, you should strongly consider getting an attorney to put you both on an even playing field.

Who Are the Best Candidates to Use the Domestic Relations Forms?

Generally, simple uncontested cases of any kind are the best candidates to use the Dom. Rel. forms. As discussed previously, cases are uncontested when both parties agree on the outcome. If you have a contested case, it may become an uncontested case if you successfully use mediation to solve the problem before you come to court. Some examples of uncontested cases include: divorces where there is no property, no children involved, and the parties have been separated two or more years; divorces where the parties have already signed a separation agreement dealing with all the issues; divorces where the parties agree to how the property and/or custody issues should be decided; custody or visitation cases where the parties already agree; custody or visitation cases where the parties have signed an agreement by using a mediator; child support cases where the parties have computed the payments using the child support guidelines; child support modifications where one party has recently lost a job; and child support modifications where a child has recently reached the age of 18.

If You Decide to Use the Domestic Relations Forms, Where Can You Get Help With Them?

There are several sources of help with the Dom. Rel. forms. Several of the Circuit Courts (Anne Arundel, Baltimore City, Baltimore County, Harford County, and Montgomery County) currently have attorneys and paralegals available to help with the forms. In Baltimore City Circuit Court and Baltimore County Circuit Court, law students from the area's law schools provide brief legal information and legal advice services on a first-come, first-served basis several times a week. Ask the clerk's office when you pick up the forms if such a service is available in the courthouse or elsewhere in your area.

The Women's Law Center of Maryland offers a state-wide legal *Pro Se* Forms Help Line that is specifically meant to help with questions on the Dom. Rel. *pro se* forms only. Currently the Help Line is operating Tuesdays and Wednesdays (9:00 A.M. to 12:30 P.M.) and Thursdays (9:00 A.M. to 4:00 P.M.). The phone number is 1-800-818-9888.

Additionally, if you have any questions about the law (not the forms), the Women's Law Center also offers a Family Law Hotline for individuals who qualify financially. Your income must be within the range set by the Maryland Legal Services Corporation, the state-wide agency that provides funding to legal service programs that serve low-income individuals. This hotline is staffed by attorneys and operates on Tuesdays (9:00 A.M. to 4:00 P.M.) only; phone 1-800-845-8550.

In Montgomery County, the Commission for Women Counseling and Career Center offers regularly scheduled legal seminars conducted by family law attorneys, covering the basic legal issues and steps in separation and divorce, and including an optional tour of the court.

If you have access to the internet you can get your questions answered by e-mail at: http://www.divorcelawinfo.com, for a modest fee per question.

If You Decide to Use the Domestic Relations Forms, Are You Stuck With Them?

The short answer is no. However, if you find an attorney represents the other side or if your case is really contested, you should seek an attorney as soon as possible. Don't expect the court to be sympathetic and let you get a continuance to find an attorney. While you may be able to save some attorney's fees by filing the Dom. Rel. forms and getting an attorney later, this would not be advisable in contested cases. The Dom. Rel. forms were drafted with the intent that only those with simple uncontested matters would be using them. Your case may require more careful drafting of the complaint or petition/motion if it is complicated or contested.

The Trouble With Being Your Own Lawyer

There are problems with trying to be your own lawyer, as there are in all legal cases. There are court procedures that must be followed in any legal action, one of which, for example, is known as *service*. Service has to be administered in the correct legal manner; if it is not, you might have to go back and file a new action.

There are other important considerations, such as whether or not you will have a Marital Separation Agreement; whether alimony rights are to be waived; whether you are in the proper jurisdiction; and whether you fulfill all the legal requirements for getting a divorce. Even if you are firm about representing yourself, it would be best to check with a lawyer to make sure that you have everything in order. Only a lawyer can give you specific legal advice suited to your particular circumstances. Finally, laws do change, and you need to be certain that you have current and accurate information.

Mediation: The Other Alternative

When you and your spouse can't agree on certain critical issues, your first alternative to the traditional adversarial system should be mediation. If you have a conflict, mediation is the path to take to avoid litigation and the adversarial model.

Until the last 10 years or so, just about the only course for divorcing couples was to hire lawyers to do battle for them. Often the spouses wouldn't even speak with each other, "communicating" only through their attorneys. And attorneys proliferated. The addition of "no fault" to divorce laws has given rise to an emerging alternative for divorcing couples: mediation. **Mediation** is the process in which the divorcing couple works out its problems, disagreements, and marital issues with a trained, impartial third party—the mediator. The mediator assists the couple in resolving their differences in a constructive way to reach a "win-win" decision rather than the adversarial "win-lose" situation.

What is Mediation?

The mediator may be a marriage counselor, social worker, psychologist, or lawyer trained in family and divorce mediation. At present, mediation is still open turf for any of the above professions to claim. Maryland does not have any licensing requirements for mediators. At any rate, the mediator should have received formal training from a recognized program or institute, such as the Academy of Family Mediators. They should be versed in family budgeting, the law, tax consequences of divorce, and a variety of options and alternatives crucial to contemplating divorce.

The Mediator

The major differences between a mediator and a lawyer are that the mediator assists you and your spouse in working out your disagreements together; emphasizes the restructuring of the family from a practical point of view, in addition to the legal side; pays more attention to your emotional needs; and is impartial, representing neither you nor your spouse, but both. Unlike the legal adversarial system, mediation is more sensitive to

How the Mediator Can Help

the integrity of the marriage. It tries to build on the strengths of the relationship, avoiding the "we'll get you" attitude so common with the adversarial position.

How Mediation Works

As one mediator described the process, "Mediation is neither therapy, nor the law—it's an educational process." Usually, the couple attends an orientation session in which the mediator thoroughly explains the process of mediation, such as what the couple should focus on, how they should speak to each other (keep raised voices down), and so on. The session may last for two hours.

After the initial session, the couple attends three to eight one-and-a-half- to two-hour sessions in which the mediator guides them toward making their own decisions on how they wish to end their marriage. They analyze their budgets and needs, divide marital property, review their children's needs, and reorganize their family and life-style to fit its new structure.

Mediators place special emphasis on providing an acceptable form of continuity where children are concerned and may even include children in the sessions if warranted.

The process allows the parties to analyze their situations and to understand each other's needs as well as those of the children. It may alleviate the anger and bitterness that the couples initially may feel toward each other. It also makes the couple realize that although they may not be husband and wife, they are still parents. It encourages their cooperation with each other in determining their relationship with their children.

Once the couple decides on what they wish to do, the mediator draws up a memorandum of understanding that specifies what issues have been resolved. This statement is then given to the couple's respective attorneys, who will draw up a formal separation agreement based on the statement. Please note that many mediators are not lawyers and, therefore, may not consider all that should be necessary for a good separation agreement.

The Cost of Mediation

The cost of mediation varies from $100 to as much as $250 a session. (Attorneys who are mediators usually charge more than non-attorneys do.) It usually is requested that both parties contribute to the costs, eliminating any possible feelings that the one who pays may be getting preferred treatment. Sessions also may be held with co-mediators, a lawyer and a social worker, for example.

Does Mediation Work?

Statistics show that court-ordered child support and alimony payments tend to lag after two years and tend to be ignored entirely after five years. Experience so far has shown that people tend to abide by agreements reached through mediation.

Where to Get More Information About Mediation

Your first stop should be http://www.mediate-net.org if you have access to the internet. This Website is operated by the University of Maryland School of Law. The Website deals specifically with Maryland mediation resources and contains an on-line directory of family mediators in Maryland. This Website also offers a free on-line mediation service for spouses who are separated by time and distance, such as parents who are fighting about custody or visitation and one parent lives in California, while the custodial parent lives in

Maryland. This is an experimental program and at the time of publication of this book, much of the cost of mediation is absorbed by the foundation grant.

The following is a partial list of places to turn to in locating mediators. You also should check with your local state bar associations, which may have special mediation programs sct up, such as Montgomery County Bar Association's "Voluntary Arbitration" program.

Assistance in Locating a Mediator

Family and Child Associates
414 Hungerford Drive, Rockville, Maryland

Family Center for Mediation and Counseling
Kensington, Maryland

National Center for Mediation and Education
Annapolis, Maryland

National Legal Resource Center for Child Advocacy and Protection
c/o American Bar Association, 1800 M Street NW, Washington, D.C.

Divorce, Separation, & Annulment

Jurisdiction   The same trio of actors involved in your marriage play a role in your divorce: you, your spouse, and the state. You can't simply break up, saddle your charger, and ride off into halcyon horizons. Among other legal considerations, the law limits the authority of the court to grant divorces (known as a question of jurisdiction—can this court hear this divorce?). The law also dictates when the court has jurisdiction over a divorce proceeding. You must also have a ground for your divorce that is based in Maryland law.

Within Maryland, the Circuit Courts have jurisdiction to hear divorce cases. After you gather all relevant information and papers, and give it to the court, it will decide whether it has been given the power to decide on your divorce.

After that, your spouse has 30 days (if your spouse lives in Maryland), 60 days (if your spouse lives outside of Maryland, but in the United States), or 90 days (if your spouse lives outside the United States) to respond to your request for divorce (known as a Complaint). If your spouse fails to respond, the court will proceed with the divorce. If your spouse does respond, then you and your corroborative witness will have to appear before the court in a hearing set up by the court. If your spouse answers or shows up, then after your corroborative witness testifies and you have presented other evidence, your spouse will also have a chance to do the same. The court will decide at some later time (normally 30 days after the hearing) to grant a divorce and a settlement of marital issues.

Residency   In order to start the divorce process you must file a complaint in the Circuit Court where you live. In your complaint or at the hearing, you will have to meet the residency requirement for the ground you stated.

Divorce laws apply only to the residents of a state, and each state has its own residency requirements. For the ground of voluntary separation without cohabitation, the residency requirement is one year in Maryland. The law absolutely requires that you be a resident for the stated period of time immediately prior to and at the time that you file for a divorce.

For example, you can't have lived in Maryland for six months before moving to Nebraska for another six months and then come back to Maryland to file for a divorce. After you have filed, however, you can move anywhere in the world.

Same State, Different Addresses

You do not have to remain at the same address to fulfill your residency requirement. You can move anywhere within the state from which you are filing. All of your addresses during the period of separation should appear on your divorce forms, not just your present address. You must also be prepared to prove where you lived during the separation if requested to do so at the final hearing.

Proof of Residency

Your corroborating witness substantiates your residency; testimony is all that most courts require to verify residency. Nevertheless, cases have been dismissed and even overturned because of improper proof of residency. To be safe, bring copies of your leases with you to court if you have moved a lot.

Resident vs. Nonresident

A court may take on a divorce proceeding even if your spouse is not a resident of Maryland. If the divorce proceeding involves you, as the plaintiff, and you have gone to another state since you filed for divorce and your spouse is now living in another state, you may still have your case heard in Maryland.

How to Establish Residency

To establish residency, register to vote; get a driver's license; get a job; open charge accounts; register your car; or take out a library card. The list is endless. But whatever you do, don't maintain a residence in another state that could imply that you don't intend to remain in the state from which you file.

County Jurisdiction

In Maryland the counties govern in which court your divorce will take place. This is called **venue**. The divorce must be filed where either the plaintiff or defendant resides or where either is regularly employed or has a place of business.

Divorce, Separation, and Annulment

Divorce is the ending of a marriage as ordered by a court. In Maryland, however, you could ask for two types of divorce: *absolute* and *limited*. When the court decrees or orders an absolute divorce, it means that the divorce is permanent, permits remarriage, and terminates property claims. When the court decrees a limited divorce, it means that the divorce is not permanent, does not permit remarriage, and does not terminate property claims (although the limited divorce may settle these claims); it serves only to legalize the separation and provide for support.

Annulment establishes that your marital status never existed. The court will declare that you were never married. Because the courts rarely grant an annulment, you should think twice about using this route if you want to end your marriage. The court may look to, but isn't limited to, the legitimacy of children and the preservation of the sanctity of marriage. Because of these considerations a court will look to granting a divorce instead of an annulment.

Grounds

Over the years the Maryland legislature has enacted legislation specifying the acceptable grounds for divorce, either absolute or limited. There are different grounds for a divorce, separation, and annulment. And the waiting periods may vary depending on the ground for divorce.

Before you file for divorce on your own, you need to talk to your spouse, if possible, and find out how s/he feels about the divorce and about the issues mentioned above. This will give you an indication on how to proceed with the divorce.

Grounds for Absolute Divorce

There are six grounds for a Maryland court to grant an absolute divorce, as follows:
1. Adultery
2. Desertion (constructive and actual)
3. Voluntary separation
4. Criminal conviction of a felony or misdemeanor
5. Two-year non-voluntary separation
6. Insanity

Any one of these grounds, if proved, results in the complete dissolution of the marriage (look to each ground in order to find out how to prove that ground). You can file for divorce under more than one ground: for instance, adultery and desertion.

Grounds for Limited Divorce

There are four grounds for a Maryland court to grant a limited divorce, as follows:
1. Cruelty (against my children and/or against me)
2. Excessive cruelty
3. Desertion (constructive and actual)
4. Voluntary separation

Although any one of these grounds is enough for a limited divorce, the limited divorce won't completely terminate your marital status. To do so, you must either seek an absolute divorce or an annulment.

Types of Annulment

Two types of annulment exist in Maryland. In the first type, the marriage is declared void *ab initio*, or from its inception, as though it had never existed. You do not legally have to go to court to have the marriage declared void *ab initio*, although it's a good idea. In this case of an annulment, a marriage must be "totally void" in order for it to be considered annulled.

Totally Void Marriage

There are two characteristics of a totally void marriage: (1) the marriage possesses some defect rendering it susceptible to collateral attack (some evidence that shows the marriage never happened or should have never happened), even after the death of one or both spouses; and (2) no direct step or proceeding to annul is necessary (although the latter may be desirable).

Defects

One such defect is if your spouse was formally married to someone else and still has not divorced that person. Your marriage to this spouse is considered totally void.

Another example of a defective marriage is one between "blood" relatives. There is also a provision that a minor of 17 years of age or younger could not marry unless they met the statutory provision of the Family Law Code §2-301.

The second type of annulment is called "voidable"—you actually have to go to court and have it declared void. Annulment is available in Maryland, and in some cases it can be obtained under the name of a divorce. Along with obtaining an annulment for bigamy and for lacking age of consent, a marriage may be declared void if the parties did not really intend to marry or if they are incapacitated, as in insanity, intoxication, fraud, and duress.

Voidable Annulment

However, the court prefers not to annul, but for the parties to divorce. Also, any marriage that is expressly prohibited by statute is void by annulment.

Each ground for an absolute divorce provides its time frame for when you can bring the lawsuit against your spouse to the court. If you claim that your spouse committed adultery, you can bring the action for absolute divorce at any time. As long as you can fulfill the residency requirement (discussed below), you will have no time-limit constraint to fulfill; you could bring the suit tomorrow if the adulterous act was committed yesterday.

Waiting Periods for Absolute Divorce

In a claim of desertion, however, you may have a time-limit problem. Whether the desertion was actual or constructive, you should wait a year after the event of desertion before you file for an absolute divorce.

For a voluntary separation, you must have been voluntarily separated for at least 12 months without cohabitation (without any sexual relations) before you can file for absolute divorce.

If your spouse has been convicted of a felony or misdemeanor with a sentence of at least three years or an unspecified sentence in a penal institution, and has served 12 months of that sentence, you can then file for absolute divorce.

In a two-year non-voluntary separation, before filing for absolute divorce, you and your spouse must have lived separated and apart without cohabitation for two years without interruption.

Finally, if your spouse has been confined to a mental institute, hospital, or similar institution for at least three years, you can then file for an absolute divorce provided you have met the residency required for this particular ground.

In summary, the waiting periods are:

Summary of Waiting Periods

    Adultery: No waiting period, if required residency was established
    Desertion (constructive and actual): One year
    Criminal conviction of a felony or misdemeanor: No waiting period
    Two-year non-voluntary separation: Two years
    Insanity: Three years

Adultery is sexual intercourse between a married person and someone other than the spouse. In Maryland, neither cunnilingus nor fellatio, which the law defines as sodomy, is a ground for divorce and generally neither is considered adultery. The sexual intercourse must involve some penetration

Adultery

of the female organ by the male organ; but a "completion" of the sexual intercourse is not required.

How to Prove Adultery

Probably no such thing as a pleasant adultery case exists, because names, dates, places, paramours, and the like have to be brought out in the open. If your spouse no longer cares about what you know and is open about the affair, you're comparatively lucky. You can then catch your spouse *flagrante delicto*, which means you have your spouse in the flagrant wrong. There is still a need for a corroborative witness—a mutual friend or neighbor who has no stake in the matter except telling the court what s/he witnessed, and perhaps a detective to prove your case in court.

Most adultery cases are proven by circumstantial evidence, which means that you have to establish that your spouse had the disposition and opportunity to commit adultery.

The evidence must be clear and convincing, based upon proven facts and reasonable inferences drawn from the facts. You have to be able to prove that your spouse and his/her lover had a sexual interest in each other, sufficient time for them to spend time alone together to commit adultery, and of course, a date and a meeting place.

Public displays of affection, such as hand-holding, kissing, and hugging between the guilty spouse and the paramour are generally sufficient evidence to indicate an adulterous disposition.

Opportunity may be proven by showing that your spouse was seen entering the paramour's apartment at 11 P.M. and not coming out until 8 A.M. the following morning and that they were alone. If you can only prove disposition but not opportunity, the courts may not allow your divorce because the court may reason that it is just mere speculation. The same is true if you only show that there was opportunity, but can't prove disposition. When you think about it, this seems to make sense.

Naming the Co-Respondent

Sometimes known as a paramour, the co-respondent is the person whom you charge as having committed adultery with your spouse. The co-respondent has the right to hire a lawyer and file an answer to your complaint. Naming co-respondents can get sticky, particularly if you don't have your facts right. You might be damaging the reputation of an innocent person.

The Adulterers

Adulterers are not equal under the blanket of the law. In Maryland, adultery may impact custody if the adultery could be proven to have harmed or impaired the children. Adultery doesn't necessarily affect alimony awards in Maryland. It will, however, be a factor for consideration in awarding alimony.

Condonation

Generally, if you knew your spouse committed adultery but continued to live and cohabit with him/her, then adultery can't be used as a ground. Once you resume marital relations, after you learned of the adulterous act, the court feels that you have forgiven, or "condoned," the act. But, if your spouse starts having affairs again, you can then sue on grounds of adultery. Or, if your spouse has had several affairs and you knew of and condoned only one, you may file on adultery regarding the newly discovered affairs.

In Maryland, however, condonation doesn't necessarily bar the action for divorce; it now is a "factor for consideration."

If your spouse has been convicted, not simply charged, of a crime, that is a ground for divorce in Maryland. The conviction can be for either a misdemeanor or a felony in any state, and the spouse has to serve at least 12 months of a minimum three-year sentence in a penitentiary or penal institution. *Criminal Conviction*

For all practical purposes, desertion and abandonment are one and the same. There are two elements that have to be present in order to constitute desertion: the willful desire or the intent to desert and the cutting off of the marital relationship. In Maryland, the abandonment: must continue for 12 uninterrupted months; must be deliberate and final; and must be beyond any reasonable expectation of reconciliation. There are two types of desertion: *actual desertion* and *constructive desertion*. *Desertion and Abandonment*

When your spouse packs bags, books, and toothpaste, walks out the door, moves into another apartment, and stays there, s/he is guilty of actual desertion. The spouse voluntarily leaves and has no plans to return except perhaps to pick up a forgotten belonging. *Actual Desertion*

You also can be deserted even if your spouse doesn't leave. If your spouse's behavior is so cruel or despicable that you find yourself dialing suicide prevention, you can leave and charge your spouse with constructive desertion. Constructive desertion is basically defined as one person leaving the relationship not necessarily the home *Constructive Desertion*

The following are some cases of marital misconduct that have been applied to constructive desertion:

• Willful refusal of sex, without just cause and nonperformance of other marital duties as to practically destroy the home life. The denial of sex alone doesn't constitute desertion; the spouse also has to stop carrying out the mutual responsibilities of the marital relationship.

• Conduct that endangers a spouse's life, safety, health, and even self-respect (although an isolated assault or two will not necessarily constitute cruelty in the eyes of the court unless the act was particularly severe and atrocious).

• One spouse's failure to move if, for example, the other gets a job transfer. The exception is if one spouse's choice of domicile is unsafe or unsuitable for the other.

Your spouse has left you, spent six months chasing butterflies, and suddenly wakes up one morning and decides that you are the one after all. In good faith, your spouse shows up at your doorstep and begs you to forgive and forget. In Maryland, if you say yes, then all is well. But if you say no and refuse to even see or listen to your spouse, then, strange but true, your spouse could sue you for desertion. The waiting period would start all over again beginning with the time of your refusal. *If the Deserter Returns*

Keep in mind that "good faith" is the key. If, for example, your husband deserted you and then tried to return only after realizing how high the costs of his alimony and legal fees would be, his desire to return wouldn't necessarily be considered as being in good faith.

Insanity

Your spouse must be judged permanently and incurably insane and be confined in an institution or a hospital for a minimum of three years before filing.

To prove insanity, two or more psychiatrists are needed to testify that your spouse is incurable and that there is no hope of recovery. The court will appoint an attorney to act in the defense of your spouse who you purport to be insane, and these costs are usually borne by you. In Maryland, you also must be a resident for two years before filing.

Divorce Based on Voluntary Separation

The closest the State of Maryland has to a "no fault" divorce is what is known as voluntary separation from bed and board without cohabitation. It usually means that you and your spouse have separated after mutually and voluntarily agreeing that you no longer wish to live together as husband and wife and that there is no hope for reconciliation. Your spouse can't threaten or blackmail you into leaving; you separate because you both want to. To get a divorce on this ground, you have to be separated for one year.

There are two types of voluntary separation: one for limited divorce and one for absolute divorce. Remember that limited divorce doesn't completely end your marriage.

Separation Without Cohabitation

If your spouse wants a separation and you do not, it is still possible to file under this ground, but the wait is longer. Maryland requires two years of living apart. Whether the separation is voluntary or not so voluntary, it has to be continuous. This doesn't mean that you and your spouse can't meet for lunch or dinner on occasion, but it does mean that you can not have sexual relations with each other.

If a candlelight dinner intended to discuss your children's report cards ends up kindling your sexual desire for each other, and you follow your passions into bed, then your waiting period has to start all over again. It will begin the day after your bedroom encounter even if you have been on good behavior for 11½ months. Sex between you and your spouse is strictly forbidden during your waiting period. Sex with others can be a problem, too; the grounds for your divorce could change.

You must live in separate abodes. Even if one person were to live in the attic and the other in the basement, it won't count for "living separate and apart."

In a Maryland case, a couple mutually agreed to separate. Mrs. B found a new boyfriend and everything was rosy until Mr. B asked her to share their attorneys' fees. She refused, so Mr. B got back at her. He hired a detective who spent the night watching the boyfriend arriving but not leaving until the following morning. Mr. B charged adultery. He won. It's a lesson to be heeded. In Maryland, it is best not to have sexual relations with others during your separation, particularly if you and your spouse are not on good terms.

Most lawyers prefer the voluntary separation cases and try to get their clients to "come around to it." There are two reasons lawyers prefer voluntary separation as a ground. First, it is easy to prove. All that is needed is the testimony of the plaintiff and the plaintiff's witness that the separation without cohabitation occurred. Second, it is a nice clean ground. There is no guilt attached and no "dirty" records that can be seen by anyone in the world. Divorce proceedings are public records and can be read by anyone anytime the court clerk's office is open.

In fact, very few divorces are granted in Maryland based upon a fault ground. Almost all divorces are based on either voluntary or involuntary separation. As a *pro se* litigant, you want your divorce to be based on the ground of a one-year voluntary separation.

Many people who, for personal or religious reasons, don't wish to obtain a full divorce can get a legal separation or "limited divorce" instead. Legal separations are very much like divorce with the major difference being that the parties can't remarry. You are, in effect, still legally married at the same time that you are legally separated.

Grounds for Legal Separation

In order to obtain a legal separation, you must meet residency requirements, grounds, and other legally prescribed laws just as you have to in a case for absolute divorce. Legal separations also can involve property settlements, alimony, and child support and custody.

The grounds for obtaining a limited divorce in Maryland are cruelty or excessively vicious conduct to complainant or minor child, desertion, and voluntary separation beyond any reasonable expectation of reconciliation. The court may require that the parties participate in reconciliation efforts.

The Maryland courts may grant a limited divorce even though you are seeking an absolute divorce. The courts also may decree these divorces forever or for a limited time only. And finally, Maryland's limited divorces may be revoked by the courts at any time upon the joint applications of the parties to be discharged. In such cases, you return to the state of being legally married.

In order to prove the grounds for legal separation, you must go through the same processes of proof as you would in a case for an absolute divorce. The courts give the same serious weight to legal separations as they do to divorce.

Proving Grounds for Legal Separation

ೞ

Q. If I leave the house can my spouse charge me with desertion?
A. If your spouse's conduct doesn't warrant your leaving, s/he may be able to sue you for actual desertion. Therefore, absent physical abuse, it would be wise to consult your lawyer before leaving home. Your own conduct is very important if you wish to succeed in getting a divorce on fault grounds of adultery and actual or constructive desertion. You must not be guilty of any misconduct that would justify the desertion. You must not consent to the desertion. If you consent, it would constitute a voluntary separation. There is a difference, however, between consenting and giving in to something you can't avoid.

Frequently Asked Questions About Divorce

Q. If I leave my spouse because of abuse, can I be charged with desertion?
A. Desertion is not a crime, so if you leave your spouse you can't be crimi-

nally prosecuted for it. If your spouse sues you for divorce on the ground of desertion, you can respond by claiming and proving that it was actually his/her abusive behavior that forced you to leave. In fact, if you have left your home in immediate response to a pattern of abuse, you have your own ground for the limited divorce called constructive desertion. Constructive desertion occurs when a party is forced to leave the home as a result of abuse.

Q. How long will the divorce take?
A. The length of time it takes to get a divorce varies from county to county and is dependent upon the type of relief sought and type of hearing that is necessary. An uncontested divorce will take the least amount of time and will be expedited by the court system under the new differentiated case management system. At the end of a year of uninterrupted non-cohabitation and no sexual relations, either party is eligible to file for divorce. After the defendant is served, and s/he files an Answer or the time for an Answer expires, the Plaintiff may request a hearing in front of a master (in counties that operate with a Master system) as soon as the master's calendar permits.

Q. Can I date while we are separated?
A. Parties can charge one another with adultery at any time and the existence of a Separation Agreement doesn't protect a party from being so charged. Any behavior on your part that would indicate "inclination" or "opportunity" could be used against you to establish adultery.

Q. Can my spouse's lawyer represent both of us?
A. Generally, it is a conflict of interest for an attorney to represent and advise both parties to a divorce.

Q. What health insurance rights do spouses and dependent children have after divorce?
A. The court has the authority to require either parent to name a child in the parent's health insurance coverage if the parent can obtain health insurance coverage through an employer or any form of group health insurance coverage, and the child can be included at a reasonable cost to the parent.

Separation Agreements

What Is a Marital Separation Agreement?

A separation agreement is a *contract* between a divorcing couple that spells out legal rights and obligations without taking any formal action in a court of law. Once agreed to, however, this document is enforceable as a contract, should its terms be breached.

It is usually a good idea to have one, although it can add at least several hundred dollars to your divorce bill. If you have considerable property as well as children, a lawyer will be an absolute necessity. Even if you don't have many possessions, a property settlement agreement may be your only assurance that you will not be eating cottage cheese with plastic forks for the rest of your life.

Ideally, a property settlement agreement should be worked out when your emotions cool down and you can look at your spouse, car, and silverware with more detachment than anger. That is the ideal, which all too often isn't the case, and thus, the necessity for a cool, controlled lawyer or mediator.

Keep in mind that an agreement spells out your legal rights without taking any formal action in a court of law. The agreement may be drawn before or after you have filed for divorce (even while you and your spouse are living together).

Important Legal Issues About Separation Agreements

The law emphasizes that such an agreement doesn't limit the parties' rights to file for either absolute or limited divorce at any time. The court reserves its power to modify any aspect of the agreement that affects children if it deems such a modification in the best interests of the child. A party may waive a claim to alimony as long as it is clear that this waiver was supported by the "consideration" required when any contract is written.

Because a separation agreement is considered to be a contract, however, under the law of contracts, specific protections for the parties exist. The agreement can be challenged in court if it can be proven that it was entered into by one of the parties under duress; if there was negligent misrepresentation; if there was an abuse of confidentiality (where the dependent party "trusts" the other party and is put at a disadvantage by that confidence or if the confidence yields what the law determines are "unconscionable" results); or if there is a finding of fraud.

A separation agreement may detail the cause of action for divorce, but most important, it spells out the couple's agreement on issues of alimony, custody, visitation, child support, costs of the proceeding, attorney's fees, use and possession or disposition of real and personal properties, and other issues relevant to working toward an understanding of the future relationship between the parties.

What Is the Value of Having a Separation Agreement?

If you are seeking an absolute divorce on the grounds of voluntary separation (mutual agreement on ending the marriage), a separation agreement is proof of this provided that it states that both spouses agreed to separate voluntarily and if before filing for divorce, both parties sign oaths (under penalty of perjury) that the information contained in the agreement is accurate.

A separation agreement may also be incorporated into a final divorce decree and then is enforceable as a court order. Keep in mind that an agreement spells out your legal rights without taking any formal action in a court of law.

The agreement may be may be written at any time: before or after filing for divorce; or while you are still living together. Keeping in mind that once you sign the separation agreement it becomes a contract enforceable in court, executing a fair separation agreement as soon as possible after separating should be your objective.

A valid separation agreement explains and settles all the issues, paving the way for an uncontested divorce. If you can enter into a separation agreement without spending thousands of dollars in legal fees you will have created the basis for a no-fault divorce. Most people in this category can easily manage as a *pro se* litigant, using the *pro se* forms contained in this book, or which are readily obtainable from the Clerk's office of the circuit court in the county where you reside. The only additional cost will be court filing fees and the cost of the master's fee for the divorce hearing. Currently, additional fees should be no more than $250.

What Is Covered by a Separation Agreement?

The property settlement agreement spells out your marital rights, including alimony, custody of children, child support, ownership of motor vehicles, division of personal property and household goods, division of any real property such as the family home or your weekend retreat, medical expenses, whether joint tax returns are to be filed, how and if charge accounts and credit are to be handled, payment of any outstanding bills, provisions for life insurance in the event of the death of the spouse who is providing spousal and child support, division of jointly held stocks or bonds, the division of any checking or savings accounts, the division of retirement accounts and pensions, who gets to keep the family dog or cat, rights to visit with the children, and any other matter that it is in your best interest to put in writing.

By having everything in writing, a separation agreement can save a lot of pain and aggravation in the event that there are any misunderstandings later.

Wording of Your Agreement

You have your agreement and you may think you know what it means when you read it, but will the court have the same understanding of it if you have to take it to them? It is critical that the agreement be clearly and precisely written.

For example, one man hired a noted attorney to draft his separation agreement. The agreement held that the man's alimony would cease if his spouse's annual salary exceeded $30,000. Her salary stayed barely under the limit. However, her income did not. She received rental income for a room in her house and additional taxable income for certain employee benefits that were not deemed salary. Neither the man nor his lawyer considered the legal distinction between the words salary and income. The man is still paying for this mistake.

Another common error in wording is "reasonable rights to visitation." What is reasonable to one person may not be so to another, and may be something else entirely to the court. The noncustodial spouse may feel a week is reasonable notice. In fact you both may agree with that, until the custodial spouse remarries and feels that nothing short of a month's notice is sufficient.

To avoid these potential problems, carefully read your separation agreement, keeping worst case scenarios in mind and asking yourself, "What if?" Make sure that the language is specific and the meaning is clear. You may need to hire an attorney to do this.

An Agreement or a Contract?

Your property settlement agreement is both an agreement and a contract. One thing you must be aware of is that it is a legal document that will bind you throughout the years and determine your rights, obligations, and responsibilities deriving from your marriage.

A separation agreement is enforceable in a court of law. If your spouse violates the agreement, you can go into court to seek a judgment for money damages for the violation of the contract. Or, you may go into a court of equity and seek enforcement under the court's equitable powers by requesting your aberrant spouse be held in contempt of court—which can result in a jail sentence (imposed or suspended), a fine, or both. Because it is a legal document, it would be wise to hire a lawyer, who would represent your best interests. If your spouse has hired an attorney, you would be smart to follow suit.

Breaking the Agreement

No contract is necessarily absolute; if you and your spouse want a change in the agreement, it is a simple matter to draw up an addendum modifying the original agreement. The agreement itself can't be broken without the consent of you and your spouse or by an order of the court. Taking your case to court doesn't necessarily mean that the changes you want will be incorporated. A great deal depends on the way in which the original agreement was written and whether or not the agreement has been brought within the divorce court's jurisdiction.

If you and your spouse have entered into an agreement in which you specifically state that the agreement is not subject to any court modification, then a court can't modify that agreement with respect to property rights. The court can always, however, modify provisions in an agreement regarding the care, custody, education, or maintenance of any minor children, as well as any provisions specifically left open to the court's review and modification.

If you and your spouse reconcile, this doesn't automatically rescind the entire agreement. However, if you can prove with evidence that it was the intent of the parties to rescind the agreement, it will be viewed as rescinded by the court. Alimony does stop when the parties live together, but the spouse receiving alimony can request it again through the court if the parties break up again.

What to Include in Your Separation Agreement

As with any agreement, the more issues you resolve in writing the better off you will be in the long run. The following issues are often settled in separation/property agreements.

Spousal Support/Alimony

Should there be alimony, or is one spouse waiving the right to claim alimony, and if so, what is s/he receiving instead? Is a waiver of alimony based on some valid consideration, such as property, or is it there because a spouse is not entitled to any? Is it modifiable by a court or is it fixed in legal concrete by the language of the agreement? How is it to be paid? Is it a lump sum payment or is it spaced out over a period of time? Is payment to be monthly or weekly? Is one spouse to continue to receive support, save in the event of remarriage? If so, how much? Is there to be a sliding scale provision for a cost-of-living increase in the amount of payments or coupled with the earning ability of either of the spouses? If the paying party gets a raise, does the support payment increase? If the party receiving support gets a raise, do the payments decrease? Does the agreement state that the court can modify support?

Be aware that the court may not modify certain matters unless the agreement specifically states that the court will continue to have jurisdiction over it. If it does not, your rights may be forever governed by the terms of your agreement. Conversely, a provision for alimony in a separation agreement is subject to modification by the court unless there is a specific provision in the agreement that states that alimony is not subject to any court modification. For example, unless specific language regarding alimony is used in your separation agreement and repeated in your final decree (Judgment), the amount of alimony you agree upon in your separation agreement will not become set in concrete.

Child Support

How much is to be paid for each child? Do the payments terminate at a certain point and time, for example, when the child reaches 18 or 21 years of age? Do the child support payments continue while the child is still in college or postgraduate type of school?

What is to be the tax treatment of the child support? There are ways of drafting the separation agreement so that from a tax standpoint the child support can be treated in the same manner that alimony is treated. That is, it can be deducted by the noncustodial spouse in his/her gross income and included in the gross income of the custodial spouse.

In the event of emergencies such as medical, dental, surgical expenses, and/or hospitalization, are there to be additional payments? If so, who is to pay? Is the cost to be split in half? Are the payments to be set or should they escalate along with the cost of living or consumer price index?

What happens to child support if the children later move in with the noncustodial spouse? Who will claim the tax exemption for the child?

Finally, do these payments conform with the Child Support Guidelines? If there is a deviation from the guideline amount, your agreement must explain why. Be aware, though, unless the amount is higher than the guideline, the court rarely deviates from the guidelines.

Will legal and physical custody both be joint? Both be sole? Will there be a combination of joint and sole? Is your visitation schedule specific? What type of rights does the noncustodial spouse have? Is it visitation at any time? Or is it on a specific day from one certain hour to another? Who has the right to have the children on holidays and vacations? How many weeks will the noncustodial parent have the children during vacation? Is the vacation to be two weeks at the beginning of the summer or one week at the beginning and one week at the end of the summer? Or is it to be longer? How many times during the week is your spouse entitled to take the children out?

Custody and Visitation Rights

Which parent makes decisions regarding the children's education (choice of schools), health (choice of doctors), summer plans (trips, camps), and general welfare? Is the other parent to be consulted? Which parent has final say? May the children be removed from the place where they are to reside? What happens if the custodial parent remarries and wants to move out of the state? If the wife remarries and she has custody, are the children to continue to bear the husband's name?

Is the noncustodial parent to pay medical and dental expenses for the spouse and children in addition to payments of support? What about health insurance? Is it to be a separate expense? How about orthodontic work? What right does the paying spouse have to be consulted with respect to which doctors or dentists are used? Is the payee to check with the payor before the selection of a doctor or dentist is made and the bills are incurred? Is a Qualified Medical Child Support Order (QMCSO) necessary?

Medical and Dental Expenses

Are there to be provisions for life insurance for the supported spouse in the event that the other spouse dies and there is no provision for the continuance of the alimony payments from the estate? The same thing holds true with respect to child support. Should there be provisions in the agreement for the supporting spouse to maintain a life insurance policy with the children as beneficiaries? When do these benefits terminate?

Life Insurance

A relatively new category of property has been recognized in the last few years and it continues to gain in scope and power. This property consists of retirement and pension funds, also known as "career assets."

Pension and Retirement Funds

They include IRA's, Keogh accounts, Social Security, and SEP plans. In order for these accounts to be considered as marital property, the funds must have been accrued by either spouse during the years of the marriage. This applies to vested and unvested funds.

First, you must determine if the particular retirement plan is divisible, and if the plan administrator will honor your agreement to divide a pension or retirement, and/or if some other form of property with value may be acceptable to you in lieu of the retirement plan.

Considerations regarding these funds include: who will receive the benefits of the retirement accounts? Should you leave it to the courts to decide? If you were to divide it between yourselves, which spouse would get the larger share? Is it to be divided equally? Is it to be divided only by the number of years that you were married? Will you accept a lump sum or are payments to be made over your lifetime? When you die, will or can the payments be bequeathed? What tax requirements accompany the division of the retirement plans? How can you protect yourself from tax penalties or assessments once a pension or retirement is divided? Will you receive your share before, during, or after your spouse receives his/her share?

Qualified Domestic Relations Order (QDRO)

Once you have decided on an acceptable plan for the division of any retirement or pension funds, it is critical that the jurisdiction of the courts be left open to enter any orders or decrees necessary to implement your plan.

All retirement and pension plan administrators will require that you produce a Qualified Domestic Relations Order (QDRO, pronounced quadro). Without a QDRO, you will not be able to receive a single cent, even if you and your spouse agreed that you are entitled to a share. A QDRO gives the receiving spouse a current and specific share of the other spouse's pension; it orders the Pension Administrator to designate a share of a pension for a spouse. To get a QDRO, you should find a competent attorney to draw one up.

Children's Education

Who pays for the college expenses of the minor children? Does this include tuition? Does this include the room and board? If room and board are included, does the custodial parent or spouse continue to receive support payments? How about books and transportation allowance to and from school? And how many times is that transportation allowance to be used? At the beginning and end of the semester? During semester breaks, vacation times, and the like? How about an allowance for the children while they are in college or while they are in high school? Is one spouse to foot the bill for summer camp, piano or ballet lessons, or for a tutor?

Marital Debts

In whose name are credit cards? Are you going to cancel your joint credit accounts? Itemize the debts and decide who will be responsible for each one. Both parties are responsible for marital debts. One of the greatest problems in divorce cases is who pays what. In most contested divorce cases, the real fight is not over the divorce, but over money.

Will You Each Keep What Is in Your Own Name or Divide It Up?

All separation agreements should spell out who will pay outstanding bills and up to what point the spouse will pay bills that have been incurred by the other spouse, along with a promise not to use the other spouse's credit. The agreement should list precisely which bills one spouse is undertaking to pay and which bills the other will pay, or should state that anything not set out as being the specific obligation of one party will be the other spouse's obligation. This clause should always include terms to protect one spouse from claims made against the other. In the event bills are not paid as agreed upon, an indemnification clause protects the party acknowledged free of liability.

To further protect yourself, you also may want to include a clause stating that the assumption of debt by one spouse is to be deemed spousal support. This caveat can be your protection if your spouse declares bankruptcy, because spousal support is not a dischargeable debt in bankruptcy proceedings.

Who Pays Attorney Fees?

Every separation agreement should indicate that each of the parties has had independent advice of counsel in the negotiation, preparation, and understanding of the agreement. It also should contain a provision for who pays attorney fees and court costs when the time comes to file for divorce. Again, there are a number of possible ways in which attorney fees can be handled. Each party can pay his/her own, or one spouse can pay a portion, if not all, of the other's attorney fees.

Who Pays Court Costs?

There are court costs and filing fees to get a divorce. Will you share the cost evenly or will one party pay? There should be a provision covering who should pay legal and court costs for the preparation of any documents necessary to enforce the agreement.

Tax Returns

Do you want to file jointly until the divorce? If so, how will you divide refund(s), taxes, interest, or penalties due? Who gets the deduction for the family home? The issue of who claims the children as dependents will relate to child-care credits and support/custody. Another essential ingredient in the separation agreement is a provision for tax returns. It may be advantageous to one spouse to file a joint tax return until the divorce, after which both parties have to file separately. Also, a provision should be included that spells out the obligation of the other spouse to file a joint tax return if requested to do so. The agreement also could cover who will pay any additional taxes as a result of the joint filing, what is to be done with refund checks, and an indemnification clause that holds the other party harmless against any liability for his/her own proportionate share of the tax.

Reconciliation

If you reconcile, do you want this entire agreement to be rescinded or only parts to be rescinded?

Jewish Divorce

If you are Jewish, you will want to include a provision for a Jewish divorce, or *Get*, as well as a provision as to who will pay for the cost of it.

Incorporating the Agreement

You can do two things with your property settlement agreement: you can stash it in a drawer somewhere, or you can incorporate it into your final divorce decree. If incorporated into the decree, it becomes a court order and is enforceable by the court's contempt powers. If you don't incorporate it into the decree, it simply becomes a contract between you and your spouse, which you would later have to sue upon in a separate action to enforce. For all practical purposes, it is easier to get a contempt charge than to file a separate breach of contract suit.

Mutual Releases

Your separation agreement should contain a provision that mutually releases all rights that you may have with one another, except the ground for divorce. Some of the rights that you are waiving are the following: all the right, title, interest, and claim that you might have or may later have as the husband, wife, widower, widow, or next of kin, successor, in and to any real or personal property you now own or may later acquire; or to participate in any way as executor of your spouse's estate.

This portion of the separation agreement should also guarantee that you and your spouse will execute any documents, such as an automobile transfer of title that may be necessary to effect any part of the separation agreement.

Legal Representation

The time and energy invested in crafting a well-considered separation agreement will pay off both financially and emotionally in the future. Since the separation agreement functions as a legally binding contract and it also details the nature of all future relations between the couple, it is advisable to consult with an attorney in crafting a separation agreement to ensure that neither party waives any rights.

The items listed above are those that you may find in a separation agreement. The list is not intended to be all-inclusive. Every case presents different questions and must be dealt with accordingly.

Sample Separation Agreements

Two sample separation agreements are given below.

A couple that does not have any property or children could use *Example 1*. It is a sample of a short agreement. *Example 2* is for a couple with children and property and is necessarily lengthier.

The agreement should be typed on standard, white, typing paper, 8½" x 11" in size. Each party's signature should be witnessed and the document notarized.

(Example 1: Without Property)

SEPARATION AGREEMENT

THIS AGREEMENT made this 15th day of September, 1997, by and between SAM SPOUSE, residing at 6900 Darren Lane, Baltimore, Maryland, hereinafter referred to as "Husband," and SARA SPOUSE, residing at 1243 Bradford Road, Bethesda, Maryland, hereinafter referred to as "Wife."

WHEREAS, the parties hereto were married on March 15, 1985, in Loveland, Colorado, and

WHEREAS, in consequence of disputes and unhappy differences which have arisen between the parties hereto, the said parties have voluntarily and mutually agreed to live separate and apart, and are now and since the 18th day of September, 1995, living separate and apart.

NOW, THEREFORE, in consideration of the premises and the mutual promises and undertakings herein contained, and other good and valuable considerations, receipt of which is hereby acknowledged, the parties voluntarily and mutually covenant and agree as follows:

1. The parties may and shall at all times hereafter live and continue to live separate and apart. Each shall be free from interference, authority and control, direct or indirect, by the other as fully as if he or she were sole and unmarried. Each may reside at such place or places as he or she may select. Each may, for his or her separate use and benefit, conduct, carry on, and engage in any business, profession or employment which to him or her may seem ad-

visable. Each shall be at liberty to act and do as he or she sees fit, and to conduct his or her personal and social life as freely and as fully as if he or she were sole and unmarried.

2. The parties shall not annoy, molest or otherwise interfere with each other, nor shall either of them compel or attempt to compel the other to cohabit with him or her, by any means whatever.

3. Except as otherwise provided herein, each party releases and forever discharges the other, his or her heirs, executors, administrators, assigns, property and estate from any and all rights, claims, demands or obligations arising out of or by virtue of the marital relation of the parties including dower rights; courtesy; homestead rights; right of election regarding the estate of the other or to take against the will of the other; right of inheritance or distribution in the event of intestacy; right to act as executor or administrator of the estate of the other; and all other similar or related rights under the laws of any state or territory of the United States or of any foreign country, as such laws exist or may hereafter be enacted or amended. Nothing herein, however, will constitute a waiver of either party to take a voluntary bequest or bequests under the will of the other.

4. Each party hereby waives, releases and discharges the other from any and all causes of action, claims or demands whatsoever, in law or in equity, which he or she may or might have or claim to have against the other by reason of any matter, cause, or thing whatsoever, except marital actions and claims founded upon the provisions of this Agreement.

5. The parties hereto will be jointly responsible for the payment of all debts incurred by the parties prior to the execution of this Agreement.

6. Each party agrees to indemnify the other from any debts, obligations or liabilities of such party, which come into existence following the effective date of this Agreement. And each party agrees to hold the other harmless from and against any and all such claims and demands which may accrue or otherwise be asserted against the other. Each party covenants and agrees that he or she will not incur any debts, obligations or liabilities on the other party's credit or do anything for which the other party could legally be liable. Each party will immediately following the execution of this Agreement, cancel all charge accounts of whatsoever nature for which the other party could be obligated, and each agrees that he or she will in the future establish charge accounts in his/her sole name only.

7. The parties further agree that the execution of this document shall in no way be considered or construed as a waiver of or bar to any cause for divorce which either of the parties may now have against the other or which may hereafter accrue, or be considered or construed as constituting a ground or cause for divorce.

8. This agreement contains the entire understanding of the parties. There are no representations, warranties, promises, covenants

or understandings other than those expressly set forth herein.

9. Each party hereto declares that he or she fully understands the facts and all his or her legal rights and liabilities; and that each believes the agreement to be fair, just and reasonable, and that each signs the agreement freely and voluntarily.

IN WITNESS WHEREOF, the parties hereto have set their hands and seals to two counterparts of this agreement, each of which will constitute an original, this _____ day_____ of, 1997.

_____   _____
Sam Spouse   Witness

_____   _____
Sara Spouse   Witness

STATE OF MARYLAND
: ss.
COUNTY OF MONTGOMERY:

On this___day of _____ , 1997 before me, a Notary Public in and for the STATE OF MARYLAND aforesaid, personally appeared SAM SPOUSE, personally known or made known to me to be the Husband who executed the foregoing instrument, and made oath under the penalties of perjury that the facts and statements contained in this document are true and that he acknowledged to me that he freely and voluntarily executed the same for the purposes named therein.
WITNESS my hand and seal

Notary Public
My Commission Expires: _____

STATE OF MARYLAND
: ss.
COUNTY OF MONTGOMERY:
On this___day of _____ , 199__ before me, a Notary Public in and for the State and County aforesaid, personally appeared SARA SPOUSE, personally known or made known to me to be the Wife who executed the foregoing instrument, and made oath under the penalties of perjury that the facts and statements contained in this document are true and that she acknowledged to me that she freely and voluntarily executed the same for the purposes named therein.
WITNESS my hand and seal.

Notary Public
My Commission Expires: _____

(Example 2: With Children and Property)

VOLUNTARY SEPARATION AND PROPERTY SETTLEMENT AGREEMENT

THIS AGREEMENT, made this 15th day of September, 1997, by and between MARY JONES, of Howard County, Maryland, hereinafter referred to as "Wife," and JOHN JONES, of Howard County, Maryland, hereinafter referred to as "Husband."

EXPLANATORY STATEMENT

The parties were married by a religious ceremony on October 1, 1985, in Howard County, Maryland. Three children were born as a result of their marriage, namely: Timmy Jones, Sally Jones and Suzy Jones, born June 1, 1988, July 1, 1990, and August 1, 1992.

Differences have arisen between the parties and they have agreed to live separate and apart from one another, voluntarily and by mutual consent, in separate abodes, without cohabitation, with the purpose and intent of ending their marriage, effective the date of this Agreement. The parties mutually desire to formalize the voluntariness of their separation by this Agreement and to settle all questions of support of themselves and each other, the property and possession rights of each, and the liabilities and obligations of each as well as all other matters arising out of the marital relationship between them.

Now, therefore in consideration of the premises, the mutual benefits arising hereunder, the covenants of each, and for the purposes of accomplishing the ends sought, the parties hereby covenant and agree as follows, all as of the effective date hereof.

1. <u>Separation and Non-Interference</u>. The parties having heretofore mutually agreed to separate and voluntarily live separate and apart in separate places of abode, do hereby expressly agree to continue to do so. Each party shall, as far as the law allows, be free from interference, authority and control, direct or indirect, by the other as fully as if he or she were single and unmarried. Neither shall interfere with or molest the other or endeavor in any way to exercise any marital relations with the other or to compel or endeavor to compel the other to cohabitate or dwell with him or her.

2. <u>Independent Counsel</u>. Each party independently acknowledges that he or she has freely and voluntarily entered into this Agreement, without relying upon any representations other than those expressly set forth herein. Each of the parties has had independent legal advice concerning this Voluntary Separation and Property Settlement Agreement prior to the execution hereof, or has been afforded ample opportunity to acquire independent legal advice prior to the execution hereof. Tom Collins has represented the Wife during the preparation of this document. Johnny Walker has represented the Husband during the preparation of this Agreement.

3. <u>Legal Fees and Court Costs</u>. Each party hereby agrees to be responsible for his or her attorney's fees in connection with the negotiation, preparation and execution of this Agreement. If either party seeks to obtain a divorce in the future, that party shall be responsible for paying the court costs necessary to obtain the divorce. If either party materially breaches this Agreement, he or she shall be responsible for the costs of the other party, including all expenses, court costs, or attorneys' fees incurred in any action that is successful for the enforcement of the terms of this Agreement.

4. <u>Child Support and Custody</u>. The Wife shall have custody of the minor children of the parties, namely: Timmy Jones, Sally Jones and Suzy Jones.

The Husband shall have liberal and reasonable visitation with the children. The Husband will pay directly to the Wife the sum of Three Hundred Dollars per month for support and maintenance of the minor children. The Husband's obligation to pay support shall terminate upon the first of the following to occur: the child's 18th birthday or the emancipation of the child, the death of the child or the death of the Husband.

5. <u>Real Property</u>. The parties currently own as tenants by the entireties certain Real Property known as 100 Main Street, Ellicott City, Maryland 21042, the marital home. Upon payment of the Fifty Thousand Dollars, the Husband shall execute a Deed in favor of the Wife.   The Wife agrees to be responsible for the mortgage payment, and for all utilities payments, real property tax payments and any other payments connected to her ownership of the real property. The Wife will be responsible for all expenses incurred with said transfer, to include deed preparation, transfer and recordation expenses. The Husband agrees to relinquish any right, title or interest in and to the real property owned by the Wife.

6. <u>Alimony</u>. In consideration of the premises, covenants and mutual releases contained in this Agreement, the Wife hereby releases and discharges the Husband, absolutely and forever, from any and all claims and demands, past, present and future, for alimony and support and maintenance, both pendente lite and permanent.

The Husband hereby releases and discharges the Wife, absolutely and forever, from any and all claims and demands, past, present and future, for alimony and support and maintenance, both pendente lite and permanent. The parties expressly acknowledge that their mutual waivers of alimony and support and maintenance herein set forth are not subject to modification by any court.

7. <u>Medical Insurance</u>. The Husband is currently covered by a policy of Health Insurance through Liberty Mutual Insurance. The Husband agrees to maintain the Wife as a beneficiary under his Health Insurance policy for Health, Dental and Prescription, until such date as Wife obtains own insurance. The Husband agrees to maintain the minor children of the parties as beneficiaries so long as he is legally able to do so.

8. <u>Personal Property</u>. The parties shall have as his or her own individual property each and every article of personal adornment including but not limited to jewelry and clothing which is now in the possession of that party.

9. <u>Automobiles</u>. Each party is driving an automobile which is paid for. That party shall have sole and individual ownership of the automobile which he or she is currently driving. Either party will sign any transfer and titles necessary to transfer title to their respective names.

10. <u>Furnishings</u>. The Wife shall have the right to all of the belongings and furnishings currently located at 100 Main Street except for the following items which shall be the sole individual property of the Husband which shall be removed from the home at the time he vacates:

1. Black and Decker power tools; 2. circular saw; 3. golf clubs; 4. weight bench; 5. John Deere riding mower; 6. hunting equipment including three rifles; 7. 1985 Villanova NCAA Men's Basketball Champion commemorative banner; 8. liquor cabinet and wine rack; and 9. home brew kit.

Except as otherwise provided herein, each party shall maintain sole and individual interest in all tangible items in his or her possession.

11. <u>Pensions</u>. The parties hereby acknowledge that the Wife has a vested interest in and to a Pension as a result of her employment with Mary Kay Cosmetics. The parties acknowledge that a portion of this pension is marital property. The Husband hereby relinquishes any right, title and interest that he may have in and to the pension plan of the Wife.

The parties hereby acknowledge that the Husband has a vested interest in and to a Pension as a result of his employment with Maryland Hunting and Fishing Emporium. The parties acknowledge that a portion of this pension is marital property. The Wife hereby relinquishes any right, title and interest that she may have in and to the pension plan of the Husband.

12. <u>Checking Accounts and Other Monetary Assets</u>. Except as otherwise provided in this Agreement, all savings accounts, checking accounts, certificates of deposit and other monetary assets presently titled in the individual name of the Husband or Wife or in his or her possession, shall be and remain the sole and separate property of the party who possesses it or in whose name the asset is titled.

13. <u>Any Other Transfer of Assets or Monetary Award</u>. Based upon consideration fully given or determination of the respective equitable situation of the parties, the Husband agrees to transfer to the Wife 100 shares of IBM stock and all other interests in marital property, as of the date of this agreement.

14. <u>Debts</u>. Except as may be hereafter provided in this Agreement, the Husband and Wife shall pay and satisfy his or her own separately or individually incurred debts, and each shall indemnify and save the

other harmless from any and all liability with respect to such debts.

From the date of the signing of this Agreement, neither the Husband nor the Wife shall incur any debt or financial obligation which is or may be binding on the other, and each shall indemnify and save harmless the other with respect to all such debts, liabilities and/or obligations. The Husband and Wife shall not pledge or use the credit of the other or complete any financial transaction which may be chargeable to the other or which may result in a lien on any of the other's property.

15. <u>Waiver of Rights</u>. Except for the right, which each of the parties hereby respectively reserves, to assert as a ground for divorce any cause or ground which either of them may now or hereafter have against the other, and except for the rights provided in this Agreement, the parties from themselves and their respective heirs, personal representatives and assigns, do hereby mutually release, waive, surrender and assign unto the other, his or her heirs, personal representatives and assigns, all claims, demands, accounts, and causes of action which either of them may have against the other, whether arising out of the marriage or otherwise, including, but not limited to, any claim arising under the Maryland Annotated Code, Family Law Article, Sections 8-201 through 8-213, any amendments thereto, and any claim against the other or against his or her property by virtue of any future change of any law of this or any other State or Federal law, subsequent to the execution of this Agreement concerning marital rights or property rights whether said change results from legislative enactment or judicial pronouncement, and they do hereby further mutually release, waiver, surrender and assign to the other, his or her heirs, personal representatives and assigns, all the right, title, interest and claim which said parties might now have or which they may hereafter have as the husband, wife, widower, widow or next of kin, successor or otherwise, in and to any property, real or personal, that either of said parties may own or may hereafter acquire, or in respect of which either of said parties had or may hereafter have any right, title claim or interest, direct or indirect, including any rights of dower, statutory thirds, halves or legal shares and widow's or widower's rights of dower, or to participate in any way in the enjoyment or distribution of any of the real or personal estate of which the other may be possessed at the time of his or her death, or any right to receive any legal right or interest whatsoever therein, including the right to administer upon the estate of the one so dying.

16. <u>Incorporation into Divorce</u>. There is nothing contained in this Agreement to prevent either the Husband or the Wife from initiating and maintaining legal proceedings for divorce, absolute or otherwise, against the other in any jurisdiction based on any past or future conduct of the other, or to bar either the Husband or the Wife from defending any such actions.

Husband and Wife shall be bound by the terms of this Voluntary

Separation and Property Settlement Agreement in any divorce proceedings, and if consistent with the rules or practice of the court granting a judgment for divorce, the terms and conditions of this Agreement, or the substance thereof, shall be incorporated into the judgment of divorce. This Agreement shall be incorporated but not merged into any decree or judgment which may be granted by a court, but this Agreement shall survive the same and shall be binding forever on the Husband and the Wife. This paragraph shall apply in any divorce proceedings whether now pending or which may be initiated in the future by either the Husband or the Wife for any cause whatsoever.

17. <u>Modification</u>. There shall be no modification, waiver, or amendment of this Agreement except by a writing signed by the person to be changed. The failure of either the Husband or the Wife to insist upon strict performance of any promise or responsibility, however, shall not be construed nor have any effect as a waiver of any subsequent default of the same or similar character.

18. <u>Application of State Law</u>. This Agreement shall be interpreted, construed, and applied in accordance with the laws of the State of Maryland which shall govern this Agreement in all respects.

19. <u>Severance Clause</u>. If any of the provisions of this Agreement are held to be invalid or unenforceable, all other provisions shall nevertheless continue in full force and effect.

20. <u>Delivery of Documents</u>. Husband and Wife shall sign, acknowledge, and/or deliver any instruments, contracts, or documents which may be reasonably required to implement his or her performance under this Agreement and otherwise cooperate to give complete effect to each of the paragraphs of this Agreement.

21. <u>Voluntary Execution</u>. The parties hereto declare that they fully understand all of the terms and provisions of this Agreement; that each has been advised of his or her legal rights and liabilities or has waived his or her right to be so advised; and that each signs this Agreement freely and voluntarily, intending thereby that this Agreement shall benefit and be binding upon the parties hereto, and their respective personal representatives, heirs, legatees, devises, distributees and assigns, and all persons claiming by or through them or any of them.

WITNESS

WITNESS

WIFE

HUSBAND

STATE OF MARYLAND, COUNTY OF HOWARD, TO WIT:

I HEREBY CERTIFY that on this ＿＿＿ day of ＿＿＿＿＿＿, 199＿, before me, the subscriber, a Notary Public of the State aforesaid, personally appeared ＿＿＿＿＿＿＿＿＿＿＿＿＿＿＿＿＿＿(Wife), and she made oath in due form of law that the matters and facts contained in the fore-going Agreement either as recitals or as agreements, including the Voluntary Separation, are true and correct as therein stated and she acknowledged the Agreement to be her act and that she has a full understanding of the terms and conditions of the Agreement.

WITNESS my signature and notarial seal.

_____

NOTARY PUBLIC
MY COMMISSION EXPIRES:_____

STATE OF MARYLAND, COUNTY OF HOWARD, TO WIT:
I HEREBY CERTIFY, that on this____day of_____, 199__, before me, the subscriber, a Notary Public of the State aforesaid, personally appeared _____, Husband, and he made oath in due form of law that the matters and facts contained in the foregoing Agreement either as recitals or as agreements, including the Voluntary Separation, are true and correct as therein stated and he acknowledged the Agreement to be his act and that he has a full understanding of the terms and conditions of the Agreement.

WITNESS my signature and notarial seal.

_____

NOTARY PUBLIC
MY COMMISSION EXPIRES:_____

Property

Property Division

When a marriage ends, the couple must divide up their property and possessions. Either the couple can agree between themselves how to do this or the court will decide for them.

What Is Property?

Property is everything with exchangeable value or anything that goes to make up a person's wealth: every interest, estate, obligation, and right. Anything that you own or that generates income is considered by the law under the category of property: your car, your furniture, money in bank accounts, retirement plans, even a business or a profession. In a divorce action, property also means what you partially own and owe money on; it includes your debts.

The law in Maryland views marriage as a relationship between partners, taking into account the monetary and nonmonetary contributions of each spouse to the family unit. This means that even if one of the partners *never* earned one dollar, that partner is considered to have contributed to the family's property (or wealth) and has rights to a percentage of that property.

In order to divide up property in a divorce action, categories of property have been established.

Marital Property

Marital property includes all property that was acquired during the marriage, regardless of how it is titled (in whose name it is). Gifts from one spouse to another are marital property if they were purchased with marital funds. Pensions and business interests that were developed by one spouse are considered marital property if they were acquired during the marriage. In fact, the only property that the court may transfer from one spouse to another is one half of a retirement plan, benefit package, pension, or profit sharing.

Non-Marital Property

Non-marital property refers to property acquired before marriage, through inheritance or by gift from a third party, excluded by a valid agreement between parties, or property directly traceable to any of these sources.

Family-Use Personal Property

Family-use personal property refers to the family home and everything in it and comes into play when there are children—particularly minor children. The court's primary goal is to enable the children to live in an environment and community that is familiar to them and will provide for the parent who has the custody of the children to continue to occupy the family home and possess and use the family-use personal property for three years after the date when the divorce becomes final.

Regardless of how the family home or the family use personal property is titled, owned or leased, the court will determine who has possession of it both during (*pendente lite*) the divorce process and in its final decree. If the partner, who doesn't have possession of the home, continues to pay all or part of the mortgage, tax, or maintenance, that party has a legal right to claim the house as his or her residence for tax purposes. If the spouse who has possession of the home remarries during the three-year period, this provision ceases to apply.

○380

Frequently Asked Questions About Family Use Property

Q. What happens if the family has been living in property which was acquired by the noncustodial parent prior to marriage or inherited by that person?
A. The Court would examine closely all facts and circumstances related to acquiring the property. It is possible that a child and custodial parent would not be allowed to continue living in the home in which they resided while the parties were living together.

Q. What happens to the family home in the case of a joint and/or split custody?
A. The court would look to the needs of each child and the specifics of the particular custodial arrangement and make a determination based on the best interest of the child(ren).

Q. If a party has custody of a child from a prior marriage, can a use and possession order be obtained?
A. No. It must be a child of the separating parties.

Q. How long can the family home be kept by the custodial parent?
A. Up to a maximum of three years from the date of limited or absolute divorce.

Q. What happens if, for example, the car is titled in one spouse's name and the other spouse is using it?
A. The court would look to see how the property was acquired to see if it still fit within the definition of family-use personal property.

Q. Can the person who has obtained a use and possession order bar the other person from the house?
A. Yes. A use and possession order grants exclusive occupancy to one party. On a practical basis, the other party may need to come to the house in conjunction with visitation.

Q. What if it isn't clear what category the property fits into?
A. The court (judge) will decide what property is to be considered marital property, in the absence of an agreement between the parties. Although the court cannot transfer the title of property from one spouse to another

(except for pensions and the like), it can award money (monetary award) to one party in compensation for the other party's retention of the property.

In the case that property falls into both categories, such as a car that was purchased in part with money from one partner's non-marital funds and in part with marital funds, then the court will determine what percentage of the car is marital property and what percentage is non-marital and factor this into the monetary award when the property settlement is decreed. (It can also order the sale of the property and division of the proceeds.) The court will also consider issues of alimony/spousal support in determining property settlement issues.

C380

Determining the Amount of the Monetary Award

The following factors will be taken into account in determining the amount of the monetary award to both parties:

1. The contributions, monetary and non-monetary, of each party to the well-being of the family.

Consider: Did you concentrate on homemaking and child-rearing to the exclusion of generating an income that would have enabled you to bring property into the marital unit? Did you put your spouse through school? Did you bring money into the marriage that you earned when single, or from an inheritance, etc.—and mingle it with family funds?

2. The value of all property interests of each spouse.

Consider: Do you or your spouse have considerable property that the court will consider non-marital and that can generate an income for you? This will affect any monetary settlement.

3. The economic circumstances of each spouse at the time that the award is to be made.

Consider: Are you unemployed? Have you been out of the job market for a number of years? Do you have assets?

4. The circumstances and facts which contributed to the estrangement of the parties.

Consider: Even though fault (adultery, desertion) are not supposed to be grounds for denial of a monetary award, there still may be some impact if the case seems pretty open-and-shut.

5. The duration of the marriage.

Consider: If you have been totally economically intertwined or interdependent for a long time, the court will view settlement differently than if yours was a 2-year marriage of individuals with similar earnings.

6. The age and physical and mental condition of the parties.

Consider: See 5. above. This situation will be compounded in a long-term marriage, particularly if the dependent spouse is sick.

7. How and why specific marital property was acquired, including the effort spent by each party in accumulating the marital property.

Consider: Details of acquisition, sources of funds, etc. Are any of these items family heirlooms or an inheritance from one spouse's side?

8. Any award or other provision that the court has made with respect to family-use personal property or the family home, and any award of alimony.

Consider: All these categories are ultimately inseparable and will be factored into the court's decision.

9. Such other factors as the court deems necessary and appropriate to consider in order to arrive at a fair and equitable monetary award.

Consider: Are there children involved? Their welfare and best interests are primary in the eyes of the court. The court will favor their not being moved out of the family home, which may mean that the family home will not be sold until the youngest child is 18 years old. This is a very different picture than if there are no children and one of the partners wants to "cash out" of the family home.

The State Family Law Code discusses monetary awards and alimony in separate sections: one deals with monetary awards, and the other with awards of alimony. Despite this, these issues are deeply interrelated and largely inseparable. Under the Code, the judge must consider evidence of the amount of income to be generated by any monetary award prior to awarding alimony.

Relationship Between Monetary Award and Alimony

Child Custody & Visitation

Introduction to Custody and Visitation

When couples divorce, the question of "Who gets custody of the kids?" is one of the most difficult and often the most emotionally draining both for parents and their children. Custody and visitation are the legal terms in court-ordered determinations of which parent the child lives with and the conditions for the child to visit the other parent. Custody and visitation are never considered to be final.

Once upon a time, mothers remained mothers in divorce cases and fathers became weekend or Sunday visitors who took their children to the zoo and dutifully returned them "home" to mother at the end of visitation periods. No more. In Maryland, the law does not favor either the mother or father. Rather, they look to the relationship of each parent with the child. Child custody is no longer the sole province of women; men can, and do, get custody as well. While grandparents and others may seek custody, there is a presumption in favor of the natural parents.

When Should You Have an Attorney?

In the event that you have a highly volatile, hostile or contested custody issue you should seek out a lawyer to represent you. Additionally, if the other parent is using the services of an attorney, it is advisable that you also have an attorney. The Court of Special Appeals has held that representing yourself is not a good enough excuse for not answering a motion by an attorney of the opposing party.

Fit and Proper

Believe it or not, the court (not you) acts as the custodian or guardian of your children. If both you and your spouse are considered unfit and improper parents, the court has the right to take your children away (declare them adoptable or assign them to a foster home). As far as the court is concerned, the welfare of the children is paramount. There is no absolute definition or rules to follow in determining fit and proper parents. The basic test is, what is in the best interests of the child?

The Best Interests of the Child Standard

Regardless of any agreement you may have reached, the court's standard for initially awarding custody is to determine the best interests of the child. In order to do this the court looks at several factors. It is important to remember, though, that no one factor carries more weight than any other.

The following list is some of the factors, but not all, the court will consider.

Which person takes care of the child? Who feeds the children, shops for their clothes, gets them up for school, bathes them, and arranges day care? Who do the children turn to when they get hurt?

Primary Care Giver

What are the psychological and physical capacities of the parties seeking custody? The court may also consider evidence of abuse by a party against the other parent, the party's spouse, or any child residing within the party's household (including another child).

Fitness

Is there a custody stipulation already drawn up?

Agreements

Who will be able to keep the child's family most intact? Who is going to let the child speak with their ex-mother-in-law, for example? Who will not penalize the child for any adverse action on the part of the other parent?

Ability to Maintain Family relationships

The decision of the court may be considered reversible error if it won't hear the child's preference. The court has the discretion, however, to interview the child out of the parents' presence. A child as young as five or six years of age may be heard, though it is rare for the court to hear from a child of less than seven years. The child's ability to tell truth from fiction and his/her maturity will be the guidelines for whether a child may be heard. A child of ten or twelve years of age is certainly entitled to have his/her opinions heard and given weight in legal proceedings about custody. Additionally, the court has the power to appoint an attorney for the child in contested cases.

Child Preference

Material opportunity, measured by which parent has the financial resources to give the child more things, is another factor to consider.

Material Opportunity

The age, health, and gender of the child are also factors that the court may take into account in deciding what is in the best interest of the child.

Age, Health, and Gender

How close do the parents live to each other? How close do they live to members of the child's extended family? Which parent lives closest to the child's school and social circle?

Residences of Parents and Opportunity for Visitation

Is there a history of one parent walking out and leaving the other parent to cope with the child and the home? Which parent left filiation when you last broke up?

Prior Abandonment or Surrender of Custody?

Is there a conflict concerning the religious education of the child?
        The factors listed above will bear on the court's decision only if shown to affect the physical or emotional well-being of the child.

Religious Views

There are several types of custody. *De facto* custody refers to who actually (in fact) has custody of the child at that time. This is physical custody and does not carry the weight of the court behind it.

Types of Custody

Temporary Custody   In order to formalize custody before you begin litigation, you should file a motion for *Pendente Lite* (meaning pending litigation) or temporary custody. Temporary custody is subject to review based on the best-interests-of-the-child standard, to be discussed below. It is not an "initial" award of custody because it is understood to be temporary pending a full hearing. In order to be awarded temporary custody you must file a request for a hearing and an order for temporary custody and support (Form Dom. Rel. 51) along with your Complaint for Custody or Divorce.

Legal vs. Physical   Custody is made up of legal custody and physical custody. A person with
Custody   legal custody has the right to make long-range plans and decisions for the education, religious training, discipline, non-emergency medical care and other matters of major significance concerning the child's welfare. A person with physical custody has the child living primarily with them and they have the right to make decisions as to the child's everyday needs.

Sole Custody   Sole custody is when both legal and physical custody is given to one parent. The child has only one primary residence.

Split Custody   Split custody is easiest to describe in a situation where there are two children and each parent obtains full physical custody over one child. Some of the considerations that may bring about this result are age of the children and child preference.

Joint Custody   Joint custody is actually divided into three categories: Joint Legal Custody is where the parents share care and control of the upbringing of the child, but the child has only one primary residence. In Shared Physical Custody the child has two residences, spending at least 35 percent of his/her time with the other parent.

Additionally, you can make your own special joint custody agreement that is any combination of Shared Physical and Joint Legal Custody. One example of this is when there is one residence for the child and the parents live with the child there on a rotating basis.

Best Interests   In order to assure the best interests of the child, the court looks very closely
of the Child   at Joint Custody agreements. The most important factor to Joint Legal Cus-
Considerations   tody that is also very relevant to Shared Physical Custody is the ability of the parents to talk about and reach joint decisions that affect the child's welfare. If you are constantly fighting over what religion or what school, the court may strike down your agreement.

Other factors include: willingness to share custody; fitness; child's relationships with parents; child's preference; ability to stabilize child's school and social life; closeness to parent's homes (primarily a factor during the school year); employment considerations (e.g., long hours and extensive travel); age and number of children; financial status; and benefit to parent.

Additionally, the sincerity of the parties involved is important. The court will want to make sure that joint custody isn't being traded for concessions on other points. Another consideration is whether the granting of joint custody will affect any assistance programs. Currently, AFDC and Medical

Assistance are affected based on the award of Joint Legal Custody. Be sure to check with your contact at any social service agencies before entering into an agreement, or you may be jeopardizing your benefits. This list is not meant to be exhaustive and the court will hear anything that they believe to be relevant.

Jurisdiction is the imaginary fence that separates the subjects one court hears from another. There are two types of jurisdiction: personal and subject matter. The court must have both types of jurisdiction to hear a case. Personal jurisdiction, the power to require a person to appear in court, is discussed in the Service of Process section of the General Instructions for completing the Dom. Rel. Forms. The Circuit Court is the court in Maryland with jurisdiction to hear matters of Custody and Visitation. To have jurisdiction over your specific custody or visitation case, the court will require one of the following: *Jurisdiction*

1. Maryland is the home State of the child (lives in State, goes to school in State) and the parent has sufficient contact with the State (works, votes, lives, pays taxes in Maryland).

2. Maryland was the child's home State within the last six months and the parent filing for custody continues to live in Maryland and the child is absent from the State because another person took him/her out of Maryland claiming custody.

3. The child and at least one of the parents have significant connection with Maryland (live, work, go to school here) and in Maryland there are more records and witnesses to give evidence of the child's present or future care, protection, training and personal relationships.

4. The child is physically present in Maryland and was abandoned or emergency protection is necessary (the child was threatened or subjected to abuse or neglect).

5. No other State has jurisdiction based on 1, 2, 3, or 4 above.

6. Another State says Maryland has jurisdiction.

7. If the child was removed from Maryland and the UCCJA (described below) does not apply and no other State has jurisdiction, then Maryland will have jurisdiction if:

a) Maryland was where the married couple lived, paid taxes, voted, etc., but the parents are now currently separated or divorced, or Maryland was where the marriage contract was last performed.

b) One parent is a resident of Maryland and was a resident when the child was removed.

c) The Court has personal jurisdiction over the parent who has removed the child.

Maryland, as well as the other 49 states, has adopted the Uniform Child Custody Jurisdiction Act (UCCJA). This act gives jurisdiction for custody cases to the location that is most closely associated with the child. Within Maryland, the Circuit Court has jurisdiction to hear child custody cases. That court has the power to override any agreement if it believes the agreement is not in the best interest of the child. *Uniform Child Custody Jurisdiction Act (UCCJA)*

*Unmarried
Cohabitants*

If the parents are unmarried, the child is considered the child of his/her mother. In order for the father to assert rights to the child (including rights to custody or visitation), paternity must be admitted or established in court. Paternity can be established by: judicial determination of paternity; the father's acknowledgment of paternity in writing; the father's open and notorious recognition of the child as his own; or by marrying the mother and then acknowledging himself as the father, either in writing or orally.

In order for a father to bring suit to establish paternity by judicial determination, he should file an action for "filiation;" but this is not required to seek custody if any of the other three methods has established paternity. Once paternity is established, neither party will be given a preference based solely on gender.

*What If You Agree
About Custody and
Visitation?*

If you and the other parent have already come to a fair agreement on the custody and visitation issue, you may want to write your own stipulation and consent order. A stipulation is a statement of the settlement that you have reached. It is accompanied by a consent order for the judge to give the agreement the power of a court decision.

Custody Agreements

If you choose to go this route, you and the other parent should be as specific as you can to avoid future conflicts. Who has legal custody? Which holiday does the child spend with you? What time and where may the other parent pick the child up? What time should the child be returned home? What is the procedure to follow if either of you are running late or won't be there on time? How much notice should you be given if they are planning a vacation? How far away may the other spouse move?

What you might think you can figure out as you go along could actually blow up into a full-scale war later. The stipulation should state everything that you have agreed upon. You should not rely on any oral promises. If you both agreed on it, write it down (no matter how trivial it may seem now). Your agreement should be included with your Complaint for Custody (Form Dom. Rel. 4), Complaint for Visitation (Form Dom. Rel. 5), or Complaint for Divorce (Form Dom. Rel. 20 or 21).

*Court Ordered
Mediation*

The court has the power to order mediation whether the custody issue is brought up by an initial proceeding, a request for modification, or a contempt action. You should be aware; however, that if the court at the initial proceeding orders mediation it will most likely prolong the legal process by stopping all other actions until the mediation is complete.

The court will initially order two sessions, but for good cause accompanied by the mediator's recommendation the court may order two additional sessions. Additionally, you may decide to continue the mediation without the court ordering it. The court also has the power to order whether one or both parties pay for the mediation. The court also has a list of court-approved mediators.

*What If You
Want to Move?*

If children are involved in your divorce case, then no matter how much you hate Maryland, you may not simply pick up and move to California. You may have to have the court's permission to do so, because your move will be denying your spouse his/her visitation rights.

It is becoming more and more common now for noncustodial spouses to insist in their separation agreements that the custodial spouse remain within a certain radius (such as 50 miles) of their former family home or that one spouse cannot take the children away for any longer than a specified period of time. In one case, a Swedish woman married to an American man was restricted from taking her child out of the country for more than six weeks. She can't simply bag it and move back to Sweden. If she does, she will be in contempt of court and could lose custody of her child.

Taxes and Custody

Usually the parent with custody can claim the exemption for the child. However, the parents may agree to claim the child exemption on alternate years. In that case, the parent with custody needs to sign IRS Form 8322, Release of Claim to Exemption. Whether or not you are taking the exemption for the child, you may still file as "Head of Household."

Visitation

Visitation is the part of the court order that defines the conditions for the non-custodial parent to have contact with the child. Visitation is limited by legal custody being vested in the other parent. This means that your visitation does not give you the authority to conflict with the long-range decisions and policies of the parent with legal custody. For example, if the parent with legal custody has decided to raise the child in the Jewish tradition, the parent with visitation rights may not take the child to be baptized in a Catholic Church.

Supervised Visitation

There are no reported cases of a court honoring complete denial of visitation for a parent. Even in cases of abuse, the only reported cases have upheld supervised visitation. Supervised visitation is when the parent is allowed to visit with the child only in the company of another person. This person is usually a friend or relative that the two parents agree will be allowed to act as a chaperone. Supervised visitation often calls for a restriction of visitation to a particular location and time.

Grandparent Visitation

Who can be awarded visitation? Obviously a biological parent can be awarded visitation. Additionally, grandparents (even if the parents weren't married or are not currently divorced) and stepparents may be awarded visitation rights. While there are no reported cases of brothers or sisters being given visitation, a strong argument could be made that it would be in the best interest of the child.

Denial of Visitation

When can visitation be denied? The court has the power to deny visitation. Normally the court will only stop visitation for a certain time or until a certain task is performed. For example, the court has previously stayed visitation until the parent met his/her financial obligation. If your spouse should deny you court-ordered visitation, you should file an action for contempt (Dom. Rel. 13). Many parents feel they have the right to stop paying child support, but they are wrong. Withholding child support will only get you in trouble and possibly arrested.

When the Custody Order Is Violated

People go into courthouses everyday telling clerks that the parent has not returned the child at the scheduled time following visitation and that they don't know what to do. When a custody order is violated the law requires the custodial parent/lawful custodian to first demand the return of the child.

Criminal Penalties

If the child is not returned within 48 hours, the visitation parent may have committed one of the following crimes:

If the abducting parent remained within the state: then the abductor can be charged with a misdemeanor and can be fined $25 or imprisoned for up to 30 days.

If the abducting parent crosses the state line: then the abductor can be charged with a felony and can be fined up to $1000 and/or imprisoned up to one year.

If the other parent has actually stolen the child, you should report this to your local police department immediately. The FBI can be called in to find the fugitive parent and the child as well. The only exception to this rule is when the child is in clear and present danger (the victim of abuse or abandonment), requiring the noncustodial parent to save them. The noncustodial parent must be ready to prove this clear and present danger and is required by Maryland law to file a petition within 96 hours. In that event, both parents will need a lawyer.

Once an incident like this has happened, you may want to consider modifying the custody order.

Modification of Custody

When a parent seeks to have the custody order changed, it is his/her burden to show the court why it should be changed. The court follows the old notion that "if it isn't broken, don't fix it." This is based on the idea that stability is best for the child unless you can show that there is something in the environment that will adversely impact on the well-being of the child.

This is not as simple as it may seem. The factors in the environment have to not just make your home as good as the custodial parent's home, but better. To do this you must show that there has been a substantial change in circumstances and that it is in the child's best interests to make the change you are proposing. If the two homes are thought to be equal, then custody will stay as it is. Remember that a temporary or *pendente lite* custody order is not a final order. You would not be required to show a substantial change in circumstances to have custody changed in the "permanent" custody order.

A child at least 16 years of age can seek a change in custody on his/her own. However, it will be the minor's burden to prove that a change of custody would be in his/her best interests at this time.

The court that made the original custody and visitation order retains jurisdiction to decide modification unless the parties and child no longer have close ties to the court and the court surrenders its jurisdiction. However, the court with original jurisdiction may refuse to hear the custody case if a child has been wrongfully taken from another state or taken without the consent of the person entitled to custody.

It still happens. A day visit with the noncustodial parent turns into a nightmare for the custodial parent. The children have been snatched, which is a crime.

Parental Kidnapping

In response to this not infrequent occurrence, the Federal government passed PKPA, the Parental Kidnapping Prevention Act. It is used in two ways: to settle custody disputes between parents who reside in different States; and to offer a bit of help in locating the missing parent through the Parent Locator Service.

Parental Kidnapping Prevention Act

In addition to the Federal government's PKPA, another law adopted by all 50 states is the Uniform Child Custody Jurisdiction Act, UCCJA. Generally speaking, UCCJA is the better legislation but PKPA takes precedence because it is Federal. A major difference between them is that UCCJA can be acted on in foreign jurisdiction cases, whereas PKPA is for domestic use only.

Uniform Child Custody Jurisdiction Act

What both these statutes are supposed to do is assist in interstate custody disputes by returning the children to the proper custodial parent. Basically, both laws dictate jurisdiction rather than any major determination of custody. For example, the two statutes would assist the court in determining what state has jurisdiction, such as the child's current home state or the child's home state six months prior to the start of a custodial proceeding. The two statutes can be quite complicated and are definitely not to be tackled by the parent alone. A competent lawyer is a must in trying to work through these laws and establish custody in inter-state cases.

೦೪೫೦

Q. How do I obtain custody of my child?
A. Either one of the separated parents may petition a circuit court in Maryland for custody of a child. If the parties cannot agree about who should have custody, the court will grant custody either solely to one of the parents or joint custody to both of the parents.

Frequently Asked Questions About Child Custody

Q. Where can I find information about missing children?
A. National Center for Missing and Exploited Children
   2101 Wilson Boulevard, Suite 550, Arlington, VA 22201
   Phone: 703-235-3900. Hotline: 1-800-843-5678.

Q. Can fathers obtain custody?
A. In Maryland, fathers can gain custody of their children. The law no longer favors one parent over the other. The parent seeking custody must meet the same criteria: What is in the best interests of the child.

Q. Can a child have input into a custody decision?
A. Courts will sometimes listen to the wishes of older children. Courts rarely take into account the wishes of very young children. Children who are 16 years or older may petition the court themselves for a change in custody.

Q. What is supervised visitation?

A. Supervised visitation means that the non-custodial parent may not spend time alone with the child. It usually also means that the non-custodial parent may visit the child at a particular time and in a particular place.

Q. When do grandparents or other relatives have custody or visitation rights?

A. Generally, the natural parents will have a presumptive right to custody. Only in cases where the parents are found to be unfit, or there are exceptional circumstances, will third parties be granted custody. At any time after a divorce, grandparents may petition the court for visitation rights.

Q. What happens if the noncustodial parent refuses to return the child to the parent with custody?

A. If a child is under twelve years of age, it is unlawful to keep that child for more than 48 hours within the State of Maryland, or to remove the child from the State of Maryland for more than 48 hours, after the lawful custodian has demanded the child's return.

Q. Are visitation rights contingent on the payment of child support?

A. No. Visitation rights may not be denied to the noncustodial parent, even though the noncustodial parent is not paying child support.

Q. How do I exercise my visitation rights, if the noncustodial parent is denying me access to my child?

A. You may seek a court order defining your visitation rights. Violation of this order will result in the custodial parent being held in contempt of court.

Child Support

Introduction to Child Support

In the last few years, legislators have been busy making new laws, rulings, and guidelines concerning child support obligations. Failure to pay child support has now become a national problem. Both parents, regardless of who has custody, are accountable for financially supporting their children.

Child Support Guidelines

To this end, Maryland has enacted child support guidelines that the courts are to follow in determining child support payments. If the court determines that there should be a deviation from the guidelines because their imposition would be "unjust or inappropriate," the court must put the reasons or findings in writing. The findings specifically must include the amount required under the guidelines; how the court order varies from the guidelines; how the best interests of the children are served as a result of the variance; and if any items of value are exchanged in lieu of money, and the worth of the items.

The guidelines are based on the actual gross annual income of each parent. Actual income is an inclusive term that means income from almost any source, including salary, trusts, rents, dividends, pensions, social security, unemployment insurance, severance pay, lottery winnings, capital gains—you name it. Alimony also is considered income for the recipient. Alimony is, however, deducted from the gross income of the spouse who pays it. Generally excluded as income are food stamps, Aid for Families with Dependent Children (AFDC), and general public assistance.

Although the guidelines apply to the gross annual income of each parent, they are not, in practice, totally applicable to the custodial parent. The court takes into consideration the time, attention and care the custodial parent gives the children and that adds up to dollars and cents. As a rule of thumb, each parent's share of child support is determined by the amount of time spent with the children. For example, if the mother spends 75 percent of her time with the children, she may be liable for only 25 percent of the support calculated by the guidelines.

Child Support Payments

Child support payments are made to the court or parent who has custody of the child, and a precise time for payment (such as every Friday) should be incorporated into your marital settlement agreement and divorce decree. Both parents should keep accurate records of when and how much child support is paid. If you're the payer, it's a good idea to pay the precise amount of the child support by check so that if your spouse gets nasty at some later date and claims you didn't pay up, you'll at least have the canceled checks as proof. If you are on the receiving end of the line, keep a log of when and how much you were paid. How child support is used is another story. The parent with custody has the right to determine how it is spent, although the legal presumption is that is spent on the children.

A parent's voluntary contributions don't reduce the parent's obligation to pay child support. You can't take your children out, buy them half the contents of a toy store or clothing department, and expect not to pay child support that week. In Maryland, if the child is disabled, the parents may be required to support the child through adulthood.

Taxes and Child Support

Child support is neither tax deductible nor taxable. Often, the only tax relief for child support payments is for the parent who can file for a dependency exemption. Obviously, both parents can't claim their children as dependents, so it has to be agreed on by you, your spouse, and the Internal Revenue Service as to who gets to claim the kids. Generally, if both parents contribute like amounts to their children's support, then the parent who has custody of the children gets to claim them as dependents. However, if the noncustodial parent contributes over half of the child's actual support requirements, s/he can claim the deduction. The IRS also requires that if the noncustodial parent is claiming the deduction, s/he must attach a copy of the agreement to the income tax form.

Establishing Child Support Payments

There are several parts to most child support orders. First and foremost, the paying parent will almost always be ordered to make a monthly money payment to the custodial parent. The order will typically read, in part, as follows:

Father (name) is ordered to pay directly to Mother (name) as and for child support of Tom and Mary, the sum of $300 per month per child for a total of $600, payable one half on the first and one half on the fifteenth day of each month, said payments to continue until each such child shall die, reach majority, become emancipated or until further order of court.

The Child Support Order

Three key aspects of the child support order follow.

1. It requires a direct monetary payment to the custodial parent: Many paying parents resent the child support order because it is made directly to the custodial parent and not the children. Because of this, some refuse to make the payments because they see it as a form of alimony. This, however, is not true. The direct payments are to be used to pay for the vital needs of the children, such as rent, food, and clothes.

2. The court retains jurisdiction to change the order: A child support order is not set in concrete but is subject to change should future conditions warrant. Thus, either parent may petition the court to raise or lower support should conditions warrant (see below).

3. Payments automatically terminate when the child reaches majority, dies or becomes emancipated: The purpose of this language is to provide for an automatic end to the support obligation when the child reaches majority or dies. However, the issue of emancipation is often in dispute and may require a court determination.

In 1990, the Maryland General Assembly passed a law making it mandatory for the courts to use child support guidelines in all cases in which child support is sought. Although use of the guidelines is mandatory, and there is a presumption that the guideline amount is the correct amount to be awarded, the presumption is refutable.

Calculating the Amount of Child Support

The reason for the implementation of the guidelines is that the General Assembly has decided that "the law and policy of this State is that the child's best interest is of paramount importance and cannot be altered by the parties. A parent has a legal obligation to provide support for the child (in proportion to their gross earnings)."

The mathematical computation to determine the guideline amount is fairly simple. And the Legislature provided a form, which must be followed:

Computation of Child Support

1. Determine the gross monthly income of each parent.
   [–] Minus: alimony and child support paid to a third party and alimony paid in this case;
   [–] Minus: medical insurance paid for the child;
   [+] Plus: alimony paid in this case;
   [–] Equals the adjusted income.
2. Add together both parents' adjusted incomes, and determine each parent's adjusted income as a percentage of their combined incomes.
3. Obtain the basic child support amount from the table.
4. Add to the table amount (if relevant):
   a) work-related child care;
   b) extraordinary medical expenses;
   c) and educational expenses;
5. Equals the total support obligation.
6. Divide the total support obligation according to the percentage total for each parent—this is the amount that is presumed to be correct, but which is rebuttable and may be overcome.

§12-204(g) of the Maryland Family Law Article provides that child-care expenses shall be added to the basic obligation. Child-care expenses should be determined by actual family experience, unless there is no actual family experience or actual family experience is not in the best interest of the child.

§12-204(h) of the Maryland Family Law Article also provides for additional support for extraordinary medical expenses including uninsured, reasonable and necessary costs for orthodontia, dental treatment, asthma treatment, physical therapy, treatment for any chronic health problem, and professional counseling or psychiatric therapy for diagnosed mental disorders.

It should be noted that there is a separate form for situations where the parents share physical custody of the children.

Monthly Child Support Obligations For Maryland

Editor's Note: The child support payment for monthly incomes of $100–$500 is $20–$50 per month, based on resources and living expenses of obligor and number of children due support. Remember, too, that this 1998 table is subject to change.

Support Guidelines Table

Combined Adjusted Actual Income	1 Child	2 Children	3 Children	4 Children	5 Children	6 or more Children
600	85	86	87	87	88	89
650	117	118	119	121	122	123
700	149	150	152	154	155	157
750	162	183	185	187	189	191
800	170	215	217	220	222	224
850	178	245	248	251	253	256
900	184	273	276	279	282	285
950	191	296	304	307	311	314
1000	198	307	332	336	340	343
1050	205	318	360	364	368	372
1100	212	329	389	393	397	401
1150	219	339	416	421	425	430
1200	226	350	438	449	454	458
1250	233	360	451	477	482	487
1300	239	371	465	504	510	515
1350	246	382	478	532	538	544
1400	253	392	491	554	566	572
1450	260	403	504	569	594	601
1500	267	413	517	584	623	629
1550	274	424	531	599	651	658
1600	282	436	546	616	672	691
1650	288	447	559	631	688	725
1700	295	457	572	645	704	753
1750	302	467	585	660	720	770
1800	308	477	598	674	735	787
1850	315	488	611	689	751	804
1900	321	498	624	703	767	821
1950	327	506	634	715	780	835
2000	332	515	645	727	793	848
2050	338	523	655	739	806	862
2100	343	531	666	751	819	876
2150	349	540	677	763	832	890
2200	354	548	687	774	845	904
2250	359	557	698	786	858	918
2300	365	565	708	798	871	931
2350	370	573	719	810	884	945
2400	376	582	729	822	897	959
2450	381	590	740	833	909	973
2500	386	598	750	845	922	987
2550	392	607	761	857	935	1000
2600	397	615	771	869	948	1014
2650	403	624	782	881	961	1028
2700	408	632	793	893	974	1042
2750	413	640	803	904	987	1056
2800	419	649	814	916	1000	1070
2850	424	657	824	928	1013	1083
2900	429	666	835	940	1026	1097
2950	435	675	846	953	1039	1112
3000	441	684	857	965	1053	1126
3050	446	693	868	978	1067	1141
3100	452	702	879	990	1080	1156
3150	458	710	8905	1003	1094	1170
3200	463	719	901	1015	1108	1185
3250	469	728	912	1028	1121	1199
3300	475	737	923	1040	1135	1214
3350	480	746	934	1053	1148	1228
3400	486	755	945	1065	1162	1243
3450	491	764	957	1078	1176	1258
3500	497	773	968	1090	1189	1272
3550	503	782	979	1103	1203	1287
3600	508	790	990	1115	1216	1301
3650	514	799	1001	1128	1230	1316
3700	520	808	1012	1140	1244	1330
3750	525	817	1023	1152	1257	1345
3800	532	827	1035	1166	1273	1361
3850	538	837	1048	1181	1288	1378
3900	544	847	1060	1195	1303	1394
3950	551	857	1073	1209	1319	1411
4000	557	867	1085	1223	1334	1427
4050	563	877	1097	1236	1349	1442
4100	569	886	1109	1249	1363	1458
4150	575	895	1120	1262	1377	1473
4200	581	905	1132	1275	1391	1488
4250	587	914	1143	1288	1405	1503
4300	593	923	1155	1301	1420	1518
4350	598	932	1166	1314	1434	1534
4400	604	942	1178	1327	1448	1549
4450	610	951	1189	1340	1462	1564
4500	616	960	1201	1353	1477	1579
4550	622	970	1212	1366	1491	1594
4600	628	979	1224	1379	1505	1610
4650	634	987	1234	1391	1518	1624
4700	639	995	1244	1403	1530	1637
4750	644	1003	1254	1414	1543	1650
4800	649	1011	1264	1425	1555	1663
4850	655	1019	1274	1437	1567	1676
4900	660	1027	1284	1448	1580	1689
4950	665	1035	1294	1459	1592	1703
5000	670	1043	1304	1470	1604	1716

Actual Income	1 Child	2 Children	3 Children	4 Children	5 Children	6 or more Children
5050	676	1051	1314	1482	1617	1729
5100	681	1059	1324	1493	1629	1742
5150	686	1067	1334	1504	1641	1755
5200	691	1075	1344	1515	1654	1768
5250	696	1083	1354	1527	1666	1781
5300	702	1091	1364	1538	1678	1794
5350	707	1099	1374	1549	1691	1807
5400	712	1107	1384	1561	1703	1821
5450	717	1115	1394	1572	1715	1834
5500	722	1123	1404	1583	1728	1847
5550	728	1131	1414	1594	1740	1860
5600	733	1139	1424	1606	1752	1873
5650	738	1147	1434	1617	1765	1886
5700	743	1155	1444	1628	1777	1899
5750	748	1163	1454	1639	1789	1912
5800	754	1171	1464	1651	1801	1926
5850	759	1179	1474	1662	1814	1939
5900	764	1187	1484	1673	1826	1952
5950	769	1195	1494	1685	1838	1965
6000	774	1203	1504	1696	1851	1978
6050	780	1211	1513	1707	1863	1991
6100	785	1219	1523	1718	1875	2004
6150	790	1227	1533	1730	1888	2017
6200	795	1235	1543	1741	1900	2030
6250	800	1243	1553	1752	1912	2044
6300	806	1251	1563	1763	1925	2057
6350	811	1259	1573	1775	1937	2070
6400	815	1266	1582	1785	1947	2081
6450	819	1271	1589	1793	1956	2091
6500	823	1277	1597	1801	1965	2100
6550	827	1283	1604	1809	1974	2110
6600	831	1289	1611	1817	1983	2119
6650	834	1294	1618	1826	1992	2129
6700	838	1300	1626	1834	2001	2138
6750	842	1306	1633	1842	2010	2148
6800	846	1311	1640	1850	2019	2157
6850	850	1317	1647	1858	2028	2167
6900	854	1323	1654	1866	2037	2176
6950	857	1329	1662	1874	2045	2186
7000	861	1334	1669	1882	2054	2195
7050	865	1340	1676	1891	2063	2205
7100	869	1346	1683	1899	2072	2214
7150	873	1351	1691	1907	2081	2224
7200	876	1357	1698	1915	2090	2233
7250	880	1363	1705	1923	2099	2243
7300	884	1369	1712	1931	2108	2253
7350	888	1374	1720	1939	2117	2262
7400	891	1380	1727	1947	2126	2272
7450	895	1386	1734	1956	2135	2281
7500	899	1391	1741	1964	2144	2291
7550	903	1397	1748	1972	2153	2300
7600	906	1402	1755	1979	2161	2309
7650	909	1407	1761	1986	2168	2317
7700	912	1412	1768	1993	2175	2325
7750	915	1417	1774	1999	2182	2333
7800	918	1422	1780	2006	2190	2340
7850	921	1427	1786	2012	2197	2348
7900	923	1431	1792	2019	2204	2356
7950	926	1436	1798	2026	2211	2364
8000	929	1441	1804	2032	2219	2372
8050	932	1446	1810	2039	2226	2380
8100	935	1451	1817	2045	2233	2388
8150	938	1456	1823	2052	2240	2396
8200	941	1461	1829	2059	2248	2404
8250	944	1465	1835	2065	2255	2412
8300	947	1470	1841	2072	2262	2420
8350	949	1475	1847	2078	2270	2428
8400	952	1480	1853	2085	2277	2436
8450	955	1485	1860	2092	2284	2444
8500	958	1490	1866	2098	2291	2452
8550	961	1494	1872	2105	2299	2460
8600	964	1499	1878	2111	2306	2468
8650	967	1504	1884	2118	2313	2476
8700	970	1509	1890	2125	2320	2484
8750	973	1514	1896	2131	2328	2492
8800	975	1518	1901	2137	2334	2498
8850	978	1521	1906	2142	2340	2504
8900	980	1525	1910	2147	2345	2510
8950	982	1528	1915	2152	2351	2516
9000	989	1539	1928	2168	2367	2534
9050	992	1543	1933	2173	2373	2540
9100	994	1547	1938	2179	2379	2546
9150	997	1551	1943	2184	2385	2552
9200	999	1554	1948	2190	2391	2559
9250	1002	1558	1953	2195	2397	2565
9300	1004	1562	1958	2201	2403	2571
9350	1007	1566	1963	2206	2409	2578
9400	1009	1570	1967	2212	2415	2584
9450	1012	1574	1972	2217	2421	2590
9500	1014	1577	1977	2223	2427	2596
9550	1017	1581	1982	2228	2433	2603
9600	1020	1585	1987	2234	2439	2609
9650	1022	1589	1992	2239	2445	2615
9700	1025	1593	1997	2245	2451	2622
9750	1027	1597	2001	2250	2457	2628
9800	1030	1601	2006	2256	2463	2634
9850	1032	1604	2011	2261	2469	2640
9900	1035	1608	2016	2267	2475	2647
9950	1037	1612	2121	2272	2481	2653
10000	1040	1616	2026	2278	2487	2659

Calculating Required Child Support Payments on the Internet

If you have access to the internet, you can calculate your child support payments by using automatic child support calculators that have the Maryland tables built-in, for either sole custody or joint physical custody. You simply go to the site, complete the form with your financial information, and click on the Submit button, and voilá you receive a calculation of the amount to be paid by both the father and the mother. The child support calculators are located at The People's Law Library of Maryland at http://www.peoples-law.com and http://www.divorcelawinfo.com.

When Support Is Not Paid

A major headache for custodial parents, children and society is created when a parent refuses to pay his or her court-ordered child support. This is a serious problem of national dimensions. A recent study found that less than half the parents awarded child support receive payment in full. This failure on the part of noncustodial parents—usually, but not always, fathers—is a major cause of poverty in children. This not only affects the families but also has an indirect impact on our society which must finance poverty programs to assist those in need.

As a result of this problem, specific laws and systems have been created to help. The custodial parent has many tools available to enforce child support orders, all of which should be considered if payments are not being made. Because child support payments are both so critical as well as so frequently delinquent, the Federal government got into the act and made it law that every state has to establish a Child Support Enforcement Agency. The law, which is part of the Social Security Act, gives the state child enforcement agencies a variety of powers to be used for collecting child support, locating runaway parents who skip child support, parental kidnapping cases, and establishing paternity and child support obligations. The law is strict and so are the agencies when it comes to dealing with absent parents who are remiss in paying their child support. Even parents who are bankrupt have to pay.

In Maryland the agency is the Child Support Enforcement Administration, Department of Human Resources, headquartered in Baltimore. Every county in Maryland has a local child support enforcement agency.

Child Support Collection Program

Originally, these child support enforcement agencies were set up to collect child support on behalf of mothers who were on welfare, and counsel were assigned to represent these clients in child support hearings and collection efforts. Today, any parent who is trying to collect child support from another parent can use the services of these agencies by simply paying a $20 fee. The fee gets you representation by counsel and the resources of the agency behind you in your child support collection efforts. The agency has strong administrative power—similar to the IRS—and usually is equally as aggressive in getting past-due obligations as well as present and future ones. It has several means to collect child support payments and does not hesitate to use them. Its job, and therefore its success, is made easier depending on the amount of information the custodial spouse gives it. Ideally, the absent parent's social security number, address, employer, and assets (bank accounts, automobiles, and property) should be provided to the enforcement agency to speed up the collection process and to locate the absent parent, if his/her whereabouts are not known. You also will have to provide the children's birth certificates, the divorce decree, separation agreement, and any court-ordered support agreement.

The agency can use a variety of sources to locate the missing parent: the state motor vehicle department, the department of revenues, the U.S. Postal Service, utility companies, and banks, to name a few.

While this agency support may seem like a good deal, unfortunately the agencies have such a backlog, that it will take time for your turn to come up. Another alternative that many custodial parents pursue is not to wait for the child support agency to represent you, but to represent yourself as a *pro se* litigant and go into court directly using the forms and instructions that are contained in this book in order to get an initial child support order. Once you get the child support order, you take it to the local child support enforcement agency, to help you enforce the order and collect the money due.

When it locates the delinquent parent, if the amount due is not forthcoming voluntarily the child support enforcement agency will use measures to collect that include the following:

Collection Measures

Obtain a Wage Assignment—Wage Withholding:

Wage Assignment

Maryland allows the court to order an employer to make direct payments to the custodial parent from the wages of the supporting parent. This procedure is known as a wage assignment or wage withholding. If the absent parent is delinquent for an amount equal to 30 days (even if s/he has made partial payments), the child support enforcement agency is required to enforce wage withholding. The wage assignment can be issued upon proper application by the court and served on the paying parent's employer. Once implemented, the employer will deduct child support like any other deduction from the paying parent's paycheck and send the money directly to the custodial parent. This is a very valuable tool—if the nonpaying parent holds a steady job.

In *U.S. v. Williams*, 279 Md. 673 (1977) the Court of Appeals had before it the issue of whether exemptions from attachment established by Com. Law. §15-601.1 were applicable to a wage lien ordered pursuant to former Art. 16 §5B (b)(1) providing for spousal support. The *Williams* Court held that the exemptions from attachment are inapplicable, because the underlying obligation is for intra-familial support. The very purpose of the statutory exemptions is to protect a family from being deprived of all support by attachment proceedings brought by an outsider.

Request a Writ of Execution:

Writ of Execution

A child support order can be enforced like other court judgments. If the nonpaying parent has assets such as real property, bank accounts, stock, a paid-off car or other property, the property may be seized upon proper application to the court. If this method of enforcing child support is chosen, a *pro se* litigant is well-advised to retain the services of a competent lawyer or pursue enforcement through the Child Support Enforcement Administration.

If the *pro se* litigant chooses to go forward on his/her own the litigant should be aware that the Maryland Rules provide a wide variety of means to execute on judgments (defined as a dollar amount that has been reduced to a judgment by the court). Rule 2-633 provides the judgment creditor with methods to use in ascertaining whether a debtor has assets and where those assets are located. Rule 2-641 provides for the issuance of a writ of execution that is used to obtain personal property of the debtor or to exclude the debtor from having access to or use of personal property. Rule 2-642 provides for the execution aspect of a writ of execution. Rule 2-643 sets out the methods used to release property. If the property seized by levy is not released by the means set forth in Rule 2-643, the judgment creditor may request that the sheriff sell the property under Rule 2-644.

If the above means of obtaining the property of a judgment debtor are not successful, other means exist. For example, Rule 2-645 provides for the garnishment of property of the judgment debtor. Generally a writ of garnishment is used when a third party is holding property of the judgment debtor. The rule states when the writ may be filed and what information shall be included in the writ. Rule 2-645 also directs the method of service to be effected and requires the person making service to mail a copy of the writ to the judgment debtor's last known address. Rule 2-646 governs the garnishment of wages of a judgment debtor.

Seizures, foreclosure, and sale are extreme measures, requiring a good deal of time, energy and money on the part of the agency. It is easier for the agency to place liens on the property rather than to seize it. A lien prevents the absent parent from selling the property until the child support owed is paid.

Unemployment Compensation Intercepts

Unemployment Compensation:
The agency also will intercept funds from unemployment from unemployment benefit checks. It has a direct line into the State employment security department.

Tax Refund Intercepts

IRS and State Refund Intercepts:
If there is at least $500 in delinquent child support payments for families (or $150 for families receiving public assistance), the child enforcement support agency will request that the IRS refund checks be intercepted. The IRS needs to know the social security number, employer or assets before it will initiate this service.

It doesn't matter if the absent parent has remarried and the refund check is issued jointly—it will be taken anyway. Likewise, the enforcement agency can intercept Maryland State income tax refund checks.

Driver License Suspension

Suspension of Driving License Privileges:
Effective October 1, 1996, if a person is more than 60 days in arrears of a child support order, the Motor Vehicle Administration will be notified by the child support enforcement agency and driving privileges will be suspended. The Motor Vehicle Administration may issue a work-restricted license or work-restricted privilege to drive in the State in accordance with §16-203 of the Transportation Article of the Maryland Annotated Code.

Credit Bureau Reporting:

If child support owed by an obligor becomes 60 days or more in arrears, the child support agency shall make available, upon request in a format acceptable to the consumer reporting agency, information regarding the arrears to all consumer reporting agencies that operate in the state.

Credit Bureau Reporting

Federal Employees:

Federal employees as well as military personnel are no longer excluded from enforcement actions when they fail to pay child or spousal support. They are subject to the same collection procedures as are others.

Federal Employee Enforcement

Bring a Civil Contempt of Court Action:

If a person willfully disobeys a lawful child support order, s/he can be jailed for contempt of court. The custodial parent brings the civil contempt action. After that, the nonpaying parent will have to be served with process since s/he has the Constitutional right to appear at the hearing and present a defense. If the nonpaying parent is served with process and does not appear, the trial court will order a bench warrant issued for his or her arrest.

Contempt of Court Action

If the court finds beyond a reasonable doubt that the parent has willfully failed to pay pursuant to a valid child support order, the court can order the nonpaying parent jailed. (A parent who can show that they did not have the ability to pay will not be found in contempt of court, even though s/he will continue to owe the money.)

Often, the mere *threat* of jail is sufficient to pry open the recalcitrant parent's pocketbook. However, in severe cases, parents will be jailed and often the jail sentence will be open-ended, terminating only when the proper payment has been made.

Seek a Criminal Prosecution:

All states also have criminal statutes on the books to punish parents who refuse to pay their child support. Although it is well-settled that an individual may not be imprisoned for a debt under Article III, Section 38 of the Maryland Constitution, a valid decree of a court of competent jurisdiction or agreement approved by decree of a court for the support of dependent children shall not constitute a debt within the meaning of the present constitutional provision. See §8-105 of the Maryland Family Law Article:

Criminal Prosecution

A parent may not willfully fail to provide for the support of his or her minor child. An individual who fails to provide support to a minor child is guilty of a misdemeanor and on conviction is subject to a fine not exceeding $100 or imprisonment not exceeding three years or both.

If the custodial parent complains to the district attorney's office, it may seek an indictment against the nonpaying parent in criminal court. If the defendant is found guilty, s/he may be jailed. Or, the guilty parent may be put on probation and allowed to remain free if s/he pays all back child support and makes all future payments in a timely manner.

Child Support Is an Enforceable Order of the Court

A child support order is as enforceable as any other court judgment or decree. Thus, a parent who is not paid child support can use each and every legal tool available to enforce the order, including wage garnishments, wage assignments, contempt of court decrees and the seizure of the non-payor's property by writ of execution.

Failure to pay court-ordered support is a contempt of court charge. The absent parent can be fined for failure to pay, or a judge can sentence him/her to jail for up to one year.

The court can also order the absent parent to a state prison to partake in a work-release program so that the parent can earn money to be turned over to the enforcement agency. Finally, the court can order the absent parent to post a bond from an insurance company that will guarantee to pay the support if the parent fails to do so.

Other Child Support Issues: Personal Jurisdiction

A court that does not have proper jurisdiction does not have the legal authority to order child support. For a court to have jurisdiction to compel a parent to pay child support, it must have personal jurisdiction over the parent. Personal jurisdiction means that the parent from whom support is sought must have sufficient contacts with the state in which the suit is brought.

Thus, if a suit is brought for child support in South Dakota and the parent from whom support is sought has only been in that State once while on vacation at Mount Rushmore, the South Dakota court would not have personal jurisdiction and would not be able to award child support—even if the children and the custodial parent lived in the State.

Courts Can Order Payment of College Expenses Even Though the Child Has Reached Majority

At one time, majority was reached at age 21. When it was reduced by law to age 18, a new problem was presented: Could the court order a parent to pay for his or her children's college expenses as child support, despite the fact that they would be over 18 when the payments were made? In most states, that question has been answered in the affirmative, if the parent has sufficient resources, although the courts are not required to make such orders.

Where the Collected Money Goes

If families have to go on state assistance such as Aid to Families with Dependent Children (AFDC), the child support that is collected, including monthly obligations as well as those that are past due (called arrearage), travels through a complicated maze, ending up in the State and Federal government coffers.

The family receiving AFDC gets some, but not all of the money. The aid is viewed as a debt and it must be paid in full before the total payments go to the family. The important thing to note is: families who receive public assistance assign all their rights to child support in return for assistance.

For families who are not receiving AFDC, the child enforcement agency will assist them in collecting their money in exactly the same manner, except the families get to keep all of it. As an added incentive for States to assist nonwelfare recipients in collecting their due, the state is paid an incentive bonus by the federal government. The bonus can be as much as 10 percent of the total collected.

Don't ignore a state enforcement agency notice if you receive one. It may not look like much, but it has more clout than you think. Respond to it within the allotted time. If you do not, you most likely will be found in default and any of the above enforcement procedures can be used against you. If you are ordered to make future payments to the collection agency, do so. Do not send them to the custodial spouse as you previously did. You may not get credit for the payments to the spouse and you may have to pay them again.

If You Get a State Enforcement Agency Notice

If your spouse has left the State of Maryland, you now can turn to the powers of the Uniform Reciprocal Enforcement of Support Act, whether or not you know where s/he is living. Every state has adopted this act, including Maryland.

Uniform Reciprocal Enforcement of Support Act

Here is how it works. The State in which you reside is called the Initiating State. The State in which the absent parent resides is called the Responding State. The Initiating State passes a set of forms to the Responding State indicating that the non-custodial parent is wanted for nonsupport. Then, if the absent parent's residence is known, the Responding State sends him/her a notice that a hearing on the support will be held. If all goes well, and s/he responds and shows up for the hearing, a new order of support will be established. The support order, however, can be for the same amount or less than the original order.

If the absent parent's residence is not known, the Responding State has to attempt to locate him/her.

This is not easy. First, the Responding State has its own cases to take care of and the volume of cases is very great. Second, each state has its own forms, laws and procedures, which adds to rather than solves the problem of child support collection. Third, the Responding State, can not be completely sure that the amount owed is valid. It only has the documents provided by the Initiating State. Therefore, the Responding State may negotiate a reduced amount of arrearage. Again, it may also issue a URESA order that lessens the amount owed. Keep in mind that the lower amount of the URESA order is valid only for the Responding State. The absent parent still owes the original amount in the Initiating State and if s/he returns to the State is still liable for the amount as well as for any arrearages. Once an order is established under URESA, the Responding State can use its powers to collect the child support.

The court that makes the original child support award is said to have continuing jurisdiction to modify the order as conditions warrant. That being so, either parent may request the court to change the order during the time the child is a minor. Modifications will not happen automatically. One of the parents must request the change by a formal motion to the court.

Modifying Child Support

Child support orders cannot be changed on caprice or because a court thinks "it is time." The change must be based on evidence proving that sufficient grounds exist to make the change. This usually requires a showing of changed circumstances from the facts as they existed at the time that the last order was entered. (In the many years a child support order re-

Changed Circumstances

mains effective, the parent's circumstances may change many times and thus so may the child support order.) In Maryland, changed circumstances means that a party's income has changed (either gone up or down) by at least 25 percent.

Many different scenarios can create changed circumstances. For example, if the paying parent has had a large increase in income, the court can order the child support increased. Or, if the child's needs grow, such as if the child becomes ill or disabled, the amount of support can be ordered raised. Sometimes the mere passage of time creates the changed circumstances. For example, as a child grows older, it becomes more expensive to buy clothes, food and other necessities. These increased expenses can be enough to justify a raise in the support order.

Support can also be reduced based upon a proper showing. For example, if the custodial parent inherits money, gets a large raise or otherwise has an increased ability to support the children, support payments may be reduced. Or, if the paying parent loses his or her job, the court can be asked to reduce support during the period of unemployment.

The Problem with Oral Agreements

A mistake many parents make is to reach informal oral agreements modifying child support. This often provides the seed for future discord. For example, the following scenario is very common:

Peter paid his former wife Alice $400 a month to support their son. When Peter was laid off, he called Alice and said, "I just got laid off. I can't afford to pay $400 right now." Alice responded, "Okay. Pay $100 for now."

Ten months later, Peter was rehired and raised his support payments back to $400. During his layoff, Peter had made 10 payments of $100. Alice called and told Peter she expected him to pay the $3,000 he had not paid during the layoff. Peter replied that he did not owe the money because they had agreed to the child support reduction during his layoff. Alice disagreed. She claimed that she had not given up the right to $400 a month but had merely permitted Peter to defer full payment until he was rehired.

When Peter refused to pay, Alice took him to court. The judge ruled that the evidence did not support Peter's claim that he was excused from $300 per month of his support during his layoff and he was ordered to pay the $3,000 to Alice at the rate of $100 a month, in addition to the usual monthly support payments.

The problem with oral agreements is that they are often vaguely worded and the memories or understanding of the parties may often differ. Thus, any agreement by parents to modify child support should be put in writing so that there are no misunderstandings later on. It is also a good idea to have a judge sign a court order based on the agreement.

The Government's Parent Locator Service

Nonpaying parents often hide from the custodial parent in order to avoid their child support obligation, often going so far as to move out of state to avoid their responsibilities. Such abandonments have caused many parents to go on welfare.

In order to attack this problem, federal legislation created the Parent

Locator Service (PLS), which allows the resources of the federal government, including the Social Security Administration and the Internal Revenue Service, to be used to locate a nonpaying parent's employer. Once found, the custodial parent or the state can enforce the child support order and collect unpaid support. The law also permits the IRS to pay child support arrears from tax refunds the nonpaying parent may be owed by the government. (The law also requires the states to establish Parent Locator Services.)

Here's how the Parent Locator Service works, or does not work, depending on your interpretation of it. The Federal legislation provides that each state may enter into an agreement with the federal government's Office of Child Support Enforcement (OCSE) at the discretion of the state. The OCSE, in turn, can provide the state with access to the Federal Parent Locator Service (PLS). The PLS contains nationwide social security information that was once used only to locate nonsupporting spouses for child support or to establish paternity. Now, however, the law grants access to the PLS for cases involving child custody in addition to parental kidnapping.

Income Withholding

Maryland law recognizes mandatory income withholding in every child support and alimony order. The law's procedures are triggered by nonpayments amounting to more than thirty (30) days of support. The law provides that the supporting parent's employer can withhold from his or her paycheck a court-ordered amount and forward it to the support recipient.

The law is intended to assist an individual, pursuing support enforcement as a *pro se* litigant (representing yourself) or with the assistance of the Child Support Enforcement Administration. As soon as payments are in arrears for 30 days, the recipient can file in court for the withholding of the other parent's wages.

A person who refused to pay child support, after being ordered by a court, also is liable to be held in contempt and could have bank accounts attached, income tax refunds withheld, and lose his/her driver's license.

೦ൟ

Frequently Asked Questions About Child Support

Q. Who is entitled to child support?
A. The parent who is separated or divorced and has custody of the children is entitled to support for the children from his/her (ex-)spouse.

Q. How is the amount of child support calculated?
A. The State of Maryland has adopted Child Support Guidelines, which have been in effect since 1990. These guidelines are used by the courts to determine how much child support the non-custodial parent should pay to the parent who has sole custody and also how much child support should be paid in a joint custody agreement. To calculate your child support obligations, go to the Child Support Calculator.

Q. I want to hire an attorney to help me enforce child support, but I don't have the money. What do I do?
A. The court can order the nonpaying parent to pay the attorneys' fees and

costs incurred in child support enforcement actions. Thus, ask the attorney you plan to hire whether s/he will defer the fee and obtain it from the nonpaying parent. Some attorneys will do this, or permit you to make monthly payments while pursuing the nonpaying parent. Others will require upfront payment in full and will reimburse you if the fees are subsequently paid by the nonpaying parent pursuant to court order. If you are representing yourself, you can apply to the child support enforcement agency in your county for assistance in establishing and collecting child support. By applying for assistance and paying a $20 fee, the child support agency will represent you as the custodial parent in a child support proceeding, irrespective of your income.

Q. How long do I have to enforce the child support order? How long may I receive child support?
A. Usually you can enforce a child support order for up to ten years. Parents are obligated to pay child support until a child reaches the age of 18. In some circumstances, a parent may be obligated to support a disabled adult child.

Q. Can I collect interest on unpaid support?
A. Yes, at the legal rate set by the State.

Q. Is there anything I can do to enforce my child support if my former spouse moves out of state?
A. In addition to the remedies mentioned above, the Uniform Reciprocal Enforcement of Support Act (URESA) permits you to complain to your local district attorney or to the local child support agency about unpaid support. The office will then contact the district attorney in the locale where the nonpaying child supporter lives. That office, in turn, will bring an action to enforce the order on your behalf. You can also register the child support order with the court in the state where the child support payor lives and then apply directly to that state for enforcement of the order.

Q. My ex-spouse is going bankrupt and owes me $5,000 in back support. Am I out of luck?
A. For the time being maybe, but not for the long run. Child support orders are not dischargeable in bankruptcy. (In fact, if your ex-spouse gets out from under the crush of debts, s/he may be more likely to pay you. At the very least, you won't be competing with a hoard of other creditors for the few dollars that may be available.)

Q. My former spouse has stopped paying support. I don't want to hurt his feelings by going to court. Am I making a mistake?
A. Enforcement of child support orders is best done early rather than late. If there is good cause to reduce payments, an agreement can be made. If the parent is merely making excuses, however, taking immediate and tough action to enforce the court order will be most likely to convince the nonpaying parent that failure to pay will have serious consequences. Moreover, if the amount owed gets too high, the nonpaying parent may never have the ability to pay it all back.

Q. How long does it usually take to enforce an order of support from a nonpaying parent?
A. Parents who refuse to pay child support are merely the tip of the iceberg of a growing U.S. problem of family discord and breakdown. It can take from 60 days to one year to enforce a court order for support, depending on whether the spouse can be located.

Q. If I remarry, must I still pay child support?
A. If a parent paying support remarries, and even if that parent has more children, s/he still must pay child support to the children from the first marriage. If a person receiving child support remarries, s/he is still entitled to receive child support unless his/her new spouse adopts the child.

Q. In a joint custody situation, may either parent still receive child support?
A. Yes. The amount of child support will depend upon the amount of time each parent spends with the child as well as the parents' incomes and the expense of raising the child.

Q. Can the court order health insurance coverage?
A. The court has the authority to require either parent to name a child in the parent's health insurance coverage, if the parent can obtain heath insurance coverage through an employer or any form of group health insurance, and the child can be included at a reasonable cost to the parent in that health insurance coverage.

Q. Do I have to pay child support to my first family?
A. Even though a parent has a second family, it does not mean that his/her responsibility to the first family goes away. The amount of the support order, however, can be affected because s/he has the responsibility for supporting another child or children. You must be notified first and given an opportunity to provide information before your support order can be changed.

Q. The other parent is in jail. Can I get support?
A. Unless s/he has assets, like property or income from an outside source or from a work-release program, it is unlikely that support can be collected until s/he gets out of jail and receives income or acquires property.

Alimony

Alimony Defined   Alimony, now often referred to as spousal support or maintenance and support, consists of periodic payments awarded to a financially dependent spouse when the couple ends their marriage. Alimony, which stems from the Latin *alimonia*, meaning "to nourish," has had such bad press that it is now referred to as spousal support.

The popular myth concerning alimony is that the wife ends up living regally in suburbia while the penniless husband is fated to a cheap hotel existence. That is far from the truth. Every study on the subject has consistently shown that it is the wife or homemaker whose standard of living drops drastically—by about two-thirds. One recent report stated the women's standard of living dropped by 73 percent, whereas the man's increased by 42 percent after the divorce.

Historically, alimony was seen as a continuation of a husband's obligation to support his wife, but now the law states that alimony may be awarded to either husband or wife, depending on each one's ability to provide for his/her own needs and the ability of the other spouse to provide for them.

Deciding the amount of alimony to be awarded a spouse can be a frustrating and complex negotiation since the legal rules are general standards that must be applied to the specific facts of each case.

Money often becomes one of the major weapons between spouses who are divorcing. Determining whether alimony will be awarded, how much, and for how long, and then securing an agreement with your spouse can be one of the most problematic and uncertain areas in divorce.

Under Maryland law, married people are financially responsible for each other—the husband has a duty to support his wife, and the wife has a duty to support her husband. Additionally, they are both responsible for one another's debts. These duties last until the final Decree in Divorce is granted; they don't stop because the couple separates.

Making Your Own Decisions   Just as with property division, you are free to make your own decisions and agreements on support or alimony as along as the decisions are the result of free and open negotiation and are fair to both parties.

If both parties have jobs and earn similar salaries, the couple may decide against any spousal support or alimony payments. In some cases, circumstances may be more complicated if one spouse is in a disadvantaged position regarding the ability to be self-supporting.

- Has one spouse been raising children and keeping house while the other has been building a business or career?
- Did one partner put the other through school?
- Are there very young children?
- Does one spouse need time to learn a skill in order to be self-supporting?

If a couple filing for divorce cannot agree on whether alimony is needed, they may ask the court to make the decision. The court will then determine whether alimony is necessary, the amount, the duration, and the manner of payment.

Alimony and Property Settlement

The Family Law Article of the Annotated Maryland Code discusses alimony and property settlement, and monetary award, in separate sections: §11-106 deals with alimony and §8-205 deals with monetary awards. In spite of this, these issues are deeply interrelated and largely inseparable. Under the law, the judge must consider evidence of the amount of income to be generated by any monetary award prior to awarding alimony.

The statutes, however, are interpreted by the courts on a case-by-case basis, and much of the current law of alimony is contained in the case law. Thus a full understanding of your alimony rights may require consultation with an attorney.

When to Seek Legal Advice

It is essential that you consult with an attorney regarding spousal support if you fall into any of the following categories:
- You have considerable personal property.
- You are a woman and have not been employed outside of the home.
- You are not capable of supporting yourself at the present time.

Types of Alimony in Maryland

There are two types of alimony in Maryland: Permanent and Temporary. Temporary alimony falls into two distinct categories: alimony during litigation and rehabilitative alimony.

Temporary Alimony

Alimony during litigation *(pendente lite)* is granted by the court before the case is even heard to cover the living expenses of the dependent spouse. This amount may be awarded for a short period or until the divorce becomes final. An award of temporary alimony does not mean that the party will be awarded permanent alimony.

Rehabilitative Alimony

Rehabilitative alimony refers to support payments for a definite period of time, sufficient for the dependent party to become economically self-sufficient. This determination may require the spouse to acquire or upgrade job skills or seek further schooling or training. At the end of this period, no further alimony will be paid.

Permanent Alimony

Permanent alimony refers to support for an indefinite period of time, terminating with the death of either party or the remarriage of the dependant spouse.

Additionally there are alimony categories that refer to whether or not, following the court decree, it is possible to alter the amounts of the alimony payments.

Technical Alimony

Technical alimony means that the amount of payments can be modified after the divorce if the agreement states that the payments are dependent upon certain conditions and the conditions warrant it. Either spouse can petition the court for an increase or decrease in payments.

Fixed Alimony

Fixed alimony cannot be modified by the court regardless of a change in circumstances. It must be stated in the agreement between the divorcing spouses that the alimony is to be fixed, or the court will understand it to be modifiable at a later date.

Alimony and the Separation Agreement

Many divorcing couples work out the thorny details of alimony and other property divisions, as well as other issues such as child custody, in a contract known as a separation agreement.

This agreement may be drawn before or after the parties file for divorce and even if they are still living together; it simply spells out legal rights and obligations without taking any formal action in a court of law. Once agreed to, however, this document is enforceable as a contract should its terms be breached by either party.

A separation agreement may also be incorporated into a final divorce decree and then is enforceable as a court order. It is advisable to work with an attorney in crafting a separation agreement that does not waive any rights or the possibility of modification of terms.

Alimony and Taxes

Even alimony has a silver lining, and this comes in the form of tax breaks. The party who pays alimony may deduct the payments from income taxes and the party who receives it as income must pay taxes on it. (Child support is not deductible but the party who pays it may take the child as a dependant on income taxes.) You can also deduct the full amount of alimony that you have paid for the year from your gross income, which will give you a lower net income on which to pay taxes. Be sure to check with your CPA or attorney to be certain you are following the rules that make alimony deductible.

If you do receive substantial alimony and it is your only source of income, you must file quarterly estimated returns so that you can spread out your tax payments over the year.

Giving Up Alimony

Once you give up or waive alimony in your separation agreement, you relinquish all claims to it forever. You might want to ask for a nominal amount of alimony, such as one or two dollars a month. If you ever need money in the event of an emergency, such as a serious illness, you might be able to ask the court to raise your alimony to cover your expenses temporarily.

Be careful that you specifically reserve your right and the court's jurisdiction, to increase your alimony award: once fixed in an agreement, alimony cannot be changed unless the agreement and decree state that it can be modified.

If the parties do not create their own agreement, the court will determine the amount of alimony based on the considerations below.

1. The financial needs and resources of both parties, including:
   * All income and assets, including non-income producing property
   * Any marital property award
   * The nature and amount of the financial obligations of each party
   * The respective rights of the parties to receive retirement benefits
   * The comparative earning power and abilities of each party
   * Whether you own your own house or any other property
   * What you owe money on
   * Whether one of you stayed home with children while the other earned the salary
   * Whether only one of you is working at a job where there are retirement benefits

   (The court will divide up a pension plan and other benefit packages in order to protect a dependent spouse.)

2. Whether you still have property, bank accounts, trust funds, stocks, etc., that you had before you got married.

   (These count as non-marital property although they will not be divided by the court in any settlement, they may be factored into your need for spousal maintenance.)

3. Whether your capacity to work outside of the home, your earning power, and your expenses will be affected by the fact that you are the primary custodian of a minor child or a disabled child.

4. The ability of the party seeking alimony to be wholly or partially self-supporting, considering:
   * Whether you ever worked outside of the home
   * Your previous salary
   * Your ability to support yourself (and partially support your children) on this income

   Whether it is more financially realistic for a spouse who is not able to earn a significant income to remain at home to care for several young children than to pay for day care for each child

5. The time necessary for the party seeking alimony to acquire sufficient education or training to enable the spouse to find suitable employment.

   (Whether it would be realistic for you to seek new training in order to gain financial independence if you could be supported financially by your spouse during the time that you were learning a new trade or profession.)

6. The standard of living established during the marriage.

   (The Court will accept a realistic change in your life-style in order to permit the establishment of two separate households.)

7. The duration of the marriage.

(The court will make the following interpretation: The longer the marriage, the greater the interdependence of the spouses and the more firmly their life-style is established, the more likely alimony will be awarded.)

8. The contributions, monetary and nonmonetary, of each party to the well-being of the family, including:

- Whether you put your spouse through school to enable that spouse to achieve the level of professional or technical training that has supported the family
- If you ran the family and raised the children to the exclusion of establishing an out-of-the-home skill or career
- Whether your homemaking let your spouse concentrate on building a career that led to economic security

9. The facts and circumstances that led to the estrangement of the parties and the ending of the marriage.

(Adultery and Desertion which are "fault" grounds for divorce in Maryland will not absolutely bar receiving alimony, but they may be a factor that the court considers in awarding or determining alimony.)

10. The age and the physical and mental condition of each party.

- An older or disabled party is more likely to be awarded support than a younger, able-bodied one
- Whether there are young children to be cared for
- If there is a reason not to consider working out of the home

(The court will not award support to a person who is capable of working regardless of their personal desire not to seek employment out of the home.)

11. Any agreements between the parties.

- Whether you and your spouse agree on property division or support issues
- If there is a separation agreement

(Even though the property settlement between parties is not the same issue as the granting of alimony, they are very interrelated. The court will consider all the resources the dependent party has, including nonmarital money and property settlement when making a decision about alimony.)

12. The ability of the party from whom alimony is sought to meet his/her own needs while meeting those of the party seeking support.

- The real financial assets that you have as a couple
- Cash on hand and assets easily convertible to cash
- The real income of the partner who is being asked to pay alimony
- The financial future of this person
- Whether income is likely to increase or to decrease over the years
- If you have non-marital resources
- Whether you expect to inherit money

Finally, to arrive at a fair decision there may be still other factors that the court considers appropriate. Because these factors derive from case law, it is often difficult for a non-lawyer to predict the outcome of a contested alimony case.

Historically, the cost of living goes up, not down. So what do you do if you are living on a fixed income of alimony payments, which is your only means of support? You could ask for an escalation agreement. Your spouse's income, like everything else, is likely to go up. You could ask for five to ten percent of your spouse's net or gross raise, if and when one is given. The argument for this is that your cost of living is going up and you need more money to meet those costs, particularly if you have children.

Escalating Alimony

You may also agree upon an escalator clause governed by the current Consumer Price Index published by the U.S. Department of Labor. To enforce this, you may put in your separation agreement a clause that states your spouse will provide you with his/her tax returns.

Once the court orders that alimony is to be paid, failure to pay is disobeying a court order, otherwise known as "contempt of court."

Enforcement of Alimony Decree by the Court

Remedies available to the person seeking alimony include: wage liens, levies upon real and personal property, garnishment of property, and garnishment of wages. It is highly unlikely that a party will be imprisoned for failure to pay alimony in Maryland.

Your Day in Court: The Hearing

Although divorce cases are a matter of public record and, as such, are open to anyone who is interested, divorce hearings, and other hearings on domestic issues, are rather private. Maryland uncontested divorce cases, and other cases such as child support, are normally heard by Masters of Domestic Relations in small, open-to-the-public courtrooms. In rural areas of Maryland, divorces may be heard by a Circuit Court judge in the courthouse.

How Do You Prepare for the Hearing?

If you are going to conduct an uncontested hearing, then be sure to go to the courthouse and observe several uncontested hearings not less than three weeks before your hearing date so that you can be familiar with the process, the different masters who might be ruling in your case, and what testimony is needed from your witness.

First, you should take some time to watch at least one case dealing with the issue that is bringing you to court. Take notes of the types of things the judge or master expects to be presented. Second, read the next section and make sure that you have prepared your witness for what to expect and that you have gathered the documents necessary.

The requirements of a hearing differ depending on the type of action. If it is a child support hearing, you must bring financial information. If it is a contested custody hearing, you may want to bring in an expert witness who can testify about the welfare of the child or children. As discussed previously, self-representation in contested matters is very difficult for non-lawyers because the rules of evidence come into play. In an uncontested case, the presentation of evidence is routine and can be described as a step-by-step procedure. The hearing for an uncontested divorce is an example of a hearing that a *pro se* litigant should be able to master without difficulty.

The Witness

All contested and uncontested divorce cases require that you have one or more witnesses, who are necessary to corroborate or verify the circumstances of your divorce case. In uncontested cases, the witness verifies your residency, your date of separation, the fact that you and your spouse are no longer living together and cohabiting, that the separation has been voluntary and continuous, and that there is no hope for a reconciliation.

Choosing Your Witness

Your witness can be almost anyone: a friend, a parent, a neighbor, a relative, even your grown children. Your witness should be someone who knows you and your situation well and, also, someone whom you can trust.

What Do You Need to Bring to the Hearing?

On the day of your hearing, be sure to bring:
- ✓—The witness
- ✓—All required forms
- ✓—Your notarized separation and property settlement agreement (if you have one)
- ✓—Your Joint Statement of Parties Conceding Marital and Non-Marital Property (a Domestic Relations form)
- ✓—Your marriage license

If You Have Minor Children

If you have minor children, bring:
- ✓—At least three recent payroll stubs
- ✓—Your last two income tax returns
- ✓—The most recent information you have on your spouse's employment and income

Uncontested Divorce or Uncontested Custody

For an uncontested divorce or uncontested custody, bring:
- ✓ Your Child Support Guidelines Worksheet

These will be required to establish child support or establish that the child support is within the guidelines. If the support is not within the guidelines, you will be asked why it is in the child's best interest that it is not. Absent a good reason, the master may recommend that the court not approve the agreement. You will need a completed copy of the Child Support Guidelines Worksheet. You can get the Worksheet from the Clerk's Office at any Circuit Court.

What Your Witness Needs to Know

Your witness must have personal knowledge of: (1) the date of separation; (2) your residence (or your spouse's) in Maryland for more than one year before the complaint was filed; and, (3) if there is no properly prepared written separation agreement under oath, personal communication with you and your spouse that the separation was voluntary, if that is your ground for divorce.

What You Will Testify To at the Hearing

At the hearing, you will need to testify as to the following:
1. Names, ages and addresses of you and your spouse
2. Date and place of marriage
3. The addresses at which you or your spouse have resided for at least one year prior to the filing of the complaint
4. The date of the separation and that you have not resided together or had marital relations since then
5. The circumstances of the separation if your ground is anything except two years living separate and apart

6. If you have children, their names, dates of birth, custodial parent, and that the custodial parent is a fit and proper person to have custody

What Your Witness Will Corroborate

You must have your corroborative witness back up what you say to prove your grounds for divorce. Your witness cannot say what you told her, but can say what she has seen and what your spouse told her.

If you are seeking a divorce on the grounds of one-year voluntary separation, and you do not have a sworn separation agreement, your witness must testify that you and your spouse voluntarily agreed to separate and how s/he knows that fact. The witness verifies your residency, your date of separation, the fact that you and your spouse are no longer living together and cohabiting, that the separation has been voluntary and continuous, and that there is no hope for a reconciliation.

Questions Your Witness Will Be Asked

The witness is asked the following questions by the master, or you can ask the questions yourself:

1. Please state your name and address.
2. How long have you known the plaintiff?
3. Where does the plaintiff live?
4. How long has the plaintiff been a resident of Maryland?
5. Did there come a time when you learned the parties separated?
6. When and how did you learn about it? (For example: They separated on May 1, 1994, and I witnessed him leaving the house with his suitcases when he was moving.)
7. Do you have occasion to visit the plaintiff?
8. How often?
9. Have you seen the defendant or any evidence of his living there?
10. Do you feel that there is any hope for reconciliation? (Reply: No, there is no hope of reconciliation.)

Questions You Will Be Asked

The following questions, with slight variations in wording, will usually be asked the plaintiff at the hearing. However, if you are *pro se*, it is a good idea to have a statement prepared giving all the necessary information in case the master doesn't ask the questions himself. Many *pro se* litigants ask themselves the questions and then recite their own answers. The sample questions, with answers in parentheses, are:

1. Please state your name and address.
2. How long have you been a resident of Maryland?
3. Has your residency been continuous? (Yes.)
4. Did there come a time when you became married? (Yes.)
5. To whom?
6. When and where was that?
7. Can you identify this document which I am handing you? (Yes, it is my marriage certificate, which I enter to the court as evidence.)
8. Were there any children born of this marriage?
9. What are their names and ages?
10. Who has custody of the children?
11. When did you and your spouse separate?
12. Where were you living at the time of separation?

13. Who left?
14. Why did you separate? (We could not get along and agreed to go our separate ways.)
15. Has this separation been voluntary, continuous, and uninterrupted for more than a year? (Yes.)
16. During the time of separation did you and your spouse resume any cohabitation? (No.)
17. Are there any property rights to be settled by the Court? (No.)
18. Is there any reasonable hope or expectation for a reconciliation? (No.)
19. Are you (or is your spouse) a fit and proper person to have custody of your minor child? (Yes.)
20. Have provisions been made for the support of your minor child? (Yes, my husband has agreed to pay me $150 a week which complies with the minimum Maryland State Guidelines based upon our incomes.)
21. Can you identify this document? (After the Maryland Child Support Worksheet is handed to you, reply: Yes, this is the Maryland Child Support Worksheet that I completed previously, which I enter to the court as evidence.)

End of Hearing

It is extremely important that neither the plaintiff nor the witness give any more information than is asked for. In many cases the divorce did not go through because people started to talk too much. Picture this question and answer: "Have you seen the defendant or any evidence of his living there?" "Well, a lot of his clothes are still there, and his stereo. And I have seen him over there a couple of times. Just a couple of months ago, he was over having breakfast with Ann." An answer like that could cause the master to stop or rescind the divorce action. This does not mean that you should lie, which is perjury. Just be sure to answer the questions simply and directly.

At the end of the hearing, tell the judge or master, "Thank you your honor," and promptly move in front of the bench so the clerk can call another case.

The Judgment

How the Decision Is Made

When a master holds the hearing, s/he makes written **recommendations** to a judge who will make the final decision. The master may prepare the divorce judgment for you. Either orally at the hearing or later in writing, the master will tell you her recommendations. If you disagree with those recommendations, you can file a **notice of intention** to file **exceptions** (a specific list of things with which you disagree) within five days after you get the master's recommendations. The master will then file a written report with her recommendations and send you a copy, and you can then file your exceptions within ten days of the day the recommendations were filed. There are other things you must do, such as get a transcript (typed copy of what was recorded at the hearing) within 30 days.

The Judgment

At your divorce hearing, you will give a copy of the written judgment that you have signed to the master unless you are told not do so. A judge will review your case and then sign the written judgment you have submitted, unless there is a problem with it. The judgment states that you are divorced and what the judge has decided about the rights of you and your spouse in the divorce (for example, you are awarded custody, your spouse is awarded visitation, and so forth). After the judge signs the document and gives it to the clerk, the judgment becomes final, and the clerk will send you a copy.

After your divorce hearing, you must fill out a blue vital statistics form the state uses to record all divorces. The form asks for your name, your spouse's name, your address, and so forth. If the master does not give you the form to fill out, you must go the clerk's office to fill out the form and give it back to the clerk. The clerk will certify your divorce and send your form to the Bureau of Vital Statistics.

Once the judgment has been signed, you should receive a postcard from the Clerk's office indicating that a Judgment of Absolute Divorce was entered on the docket on whatever date it was. That date is critical to you. For all intents and purposes, it is the day that you are legally divorced. However, the judgment does not become final until the time for taking an appeal has expired. (Of course, there should be no appeal from an uncontested divorce, since an uncontested divorce implies that there are no issues in dispute between the parties.)

After the decree is docketed there is a 30-day period in which to note an appeal. You cannot remarry until the 30 days have expired.

Until your divorce is final, your legal status is as one who is married. You should also be aware that just because you have signed the voluntary separation agreement, this does not necessarily mean that your spouse can't obtain a divorce on other grounds.

Limitations in the Meantime

You will note from the sample separation agreements (see Separation Agreement section) that there is a provision that the parties reserve the right to file for a divorce for any cause or ground that either of them may have against the other party.

Even though you may have agreed to a voluntary separation, that does not preclude your spouse from filing for a divorce on the grounds of adultery. The same could be true if a divorce was actually heard and a judgment entered. If your spouse appeals and the Court of Appeals holds that the judgment be set aside and orders a new trial, your spouse could file under a different ground, such as adultery, for divorce. This is highly unlikely, but it has happened and you should be aware of the possibility.

Your divorce can be overturned in a variety of ways, although all are quite remote. In order to overturn the judgment, the Court of Appeals must find that the person who heard your divorce acted in a manner that is "arbitrary and capricious." Defining what could be considered arbitrary and capricious might take days, but basically, it is the types of Findings of Facts that negate common sense and are extremely unreasonable. It is very difficult to overturn a divorce decision from a lower court.

How and When Your Divorce Can Be Overturned

It is best to wait 30 days after the date of your divorce judgment before you marry someone else. If you wanted to, you could remarry when the judgment is signed. However, your divorce could be appealed by your spouse within 30 days after the judgment of divorce is filed with the clerk. If your spouse appeals the divorce, the court of special appeals (the next higher court) might rule that your divorce is invalid (not legal) for some reason. If that happened, you would still be married to your first spouse and your second marriage would not be valid.

When You Can Get Remarried

Glossary Of Legal Terms

AB INITIO—Latin for "from the beginning."

ACTION—a lawsuit or proceeding in a court of law.

AFFIDAVIT—a written statement under oath.

AGREEMENT—a verbal or written resolution of disputed issues.

ALIMONY—a payment of support provided by one spouse to the other.

ALIAS SUMMONS— another summons when the original is not served on the defendant.

ANNULMENT—a marriage can be dissolved in a legal proceeding in which the marriage is declared void, as though it never took place. In the eyes of the law, the parties were never married. Each has its own grounds for annulment.

ANSWER—the paper filed with the court by the defendant responding to the plaintiff's Bill of Complaint. The answer gives the defendant the legal right to admit or deny his or her innocence. Maryland does not require an answer in a divorce case.

APPEAL—a legal action where the losing party requests that a higher court review the decision.

CIVIL DESK—that part of the Clerk's office where civil cases are processed.

COLLUSION—an agreement between two or more persons that one of the parties brings false charges against the other. In a divorce case, the husband and wife may agree to use adultery as a ground in order to obtain a divorce more quickly, knowing full well that adultery was not committed. Collusion is illegal.

COMPLAINANT—the one who files the suit, same as plaintiff.

COMMON LAW MARRIAGE—a common law marriage comes about when a man and woman who are free to marry agree to live together as husband and wife without the formal ceremony. To be common law married, both spouses must have intended to be husband and wife. Maryland does not recognize common law marriages.

COMPLAINT—called a Bill of Complaint. It is the papers the plaintiff files with the court that bring forth the allegations or reasons why a divorce should be granted.

CONDONATION—the act of forgiving one's spouse who has committed an act of wrongdoing that would constitute a ground for divorce. Condonation generally is proven by living and cohabiting with the spouse after learning that the wrongdoing was committed. It often is used as a defense to a divorce.

CONNIVANCE—one person purposely and intentionally traps the other party into committing a wrongdoing so a divorce can be obtained. For example, a husband may try to trap his wife into committing adultery by setting her up with an old lover. If discovered, connivance bars a divorce. It also is used as a defense to a divorce.

CONSIDERATION—something of value in exchange for some act or thing of value. Essential element to a contract.

CONTEMPT or CONTEMPT OF COURT—the failure of one party to comply with an order of the court, which results in punishment such as a fine or jail sentence.

CONTESTED DIVORCE—the refusal by one party to the action to agree with the other, regardless of the reason, be it grounds, custody or alimony.

CO-RESPONDENT—the person jointly charged with the defendant generally of having committed adultery. The co-respondent also becomes a defendant in the case.

COUNT—a statement of facts in a complaint or petition which is the basis for a claim.

CUSTODY—the right to care for, educate, house, and keep the children or pets. The parent having custody rights is called the custodial parent. The other parent is called the noncustodial parent.

DECREE—the decision of an equity court, as in Final Decree of Divorce.

DEFAULT—the failure to comply with an obligation or to file an answer to the complaint.

DEFAULT CASE—a case in which the defendant fails to contest the petition by filing any responsive document.

DEFENDANT—the person who has been charged in a divorce suit. The defendant has the right to admit or deny the charges. In some states the defendant is referred to as the "respondent."

DEPOSITION—an examination under oath reduced to writing used to preserve testimony or for obtaining information.

DIVORCE—a legal judgment that terminates the marriage of two people and restores them to the status of single persons.

DOMICILE—the state that you consider to be your legal, permanent home as opposed to your temporary residence.

EMANCIPATED—children are considered emancipated if they are completely self-supporting or they have married.

EQUITABLE DIVISION—a procedure for dividing marital property based on a variety of factors that seeks to allocate a fair amount of property to each spouse.

INJUNCTION—a court order called a "mandatory injunction" forbidding a party to do something such as harassment, selling property, or even ordering a party to move out of the home, enforceable by contempt.

INTERROGATORIES—written questions from one party to another in a court action, which must be answered under oath.

JOINT LEGAL CUSTODY—a form of custody of minor children in which the parents share the responsibilities relating to the child.

JOINT PHYSICAL CUSTODY—a form of custody of minor children in which the parents share the actual physical custody of the children.

JOINT TENANCY—the ownership of property with another or several persons. For example, a husband and wife who have their home in both their names, own it by joint tenancy. When one spouse dies the other automatically becomes the full owner. When the husband and wife hold title in this manner it is called tenancy by the entireties.

JUDGMENT—a final ruling or order of a court. A judgment is often called a decree.

JURISDICTION—the authority of a court to rule or preside over a particular case.

LACHES—a form of statute of limitations in which a person thinks s/he has the right to sue and would reasonably be expected to sue, but does not. For example, if a wife has lived with an impotent husband for 35 years, she would probably be denied a divorce, as laches would be put into effect.

LEGAL SEPARATION—a legal lawsuit for support while the parties are living separate and apart.

LIEN—a notice of a claim against a piece of property, warning prospective buyers that a claim must be paid from the proceeds of the sale. It can be used to collect back alimony and child support payments.

MARRIAGE CERTIFICATE—to prove that you and your spouse are married, you must have the original or a certified copy of the marriage certificate issued by the state or county where you were married. A certified copy has a raised seal placed on it by the bureau clerk certifying that it is a "true copy" of the original.

MARITAL SETTLEMENT AGREEMENT—a written agreement entered into by the spouses in a divorce that establishes future rights to property, support, and custody of children.

MASTER OF DOMESTIC RELATIONS—the judicial intermediary in Maryland who hears divorce cases and can recommend that they be granted or not.

NO FAULT—when neither party is guilty nor at blame in a divorce action.

NON–MARITAL PROPERTY—describes separate property of the spouses, usually acquired prior to the marriage or acquired by individual gift or inheritance either before or during marriage.

NOTARIZED—signed and sworn under oath before a Notary Public.

PARTY—a person directly involved in a lawsuit, either as the plaintiff or the defendant.

PENDENTE LITE—Latin for "pending the suit." It is the time prior to the suit or the time during which the suit is taking place. *Pendente Lite* alimony, child support, or custody can be awarded by the court.

PLAINTIFF—the person who initiates the suit against his/her spouse by filing a Bill of Complaint with the court. Also called "complainant" or "petitioner" in some states.

PRIMA FACIE—Latin for "at first sight." A case in which the evidence is strong enough for the defendant to answer to it.

PRO SE—Latin for "on behalf of oneself." A person who represents him- or herself in a court.

RELIEF—what the petitioner asks the court to do in his/her petition such as dissolve the marriage.

RETAINER—the initial deposit, usually nonrefundable, paid to your attorney at the beginning of your suit.

RESIDENCE—the place where a person lives, generally the same as domicile.

RESPONDENT—another term to describe the defendant in an action. The spouse from whom the divorce is sought.

SEPARATION AGREEMENT—an agreement in which the parties put in writing their intent to separate and live apart. It may also contain provisions for the division of property. Also referred to as the property settlement agreement.

SERVICE—the process by which the defendant is notified that a suit has been filed against him or her. Service may be the delivery of the Bill of Complaint by a United States marshal, by a process server, by registered return-receipt-requested U.S. Mail, or by the written publication in a newspaper that a suit is taking place. The latter generally is used only in cases of actual desertion and when the whereabouts of the defendant are unknown.

SOLE CUSTODY—a form of child custody in which one parent is given both physical custody and legal custody.

STIPULATION—a voluntary agreement between the petitioner and the respondent on the facts or law governing the case.

SUMMONS—an order issued by the court after a complaint has been filed. The summons tells the defendant that a suit has been filed and specifies the time which the defendant has to answer the complaint.

TRIAL—a formal court hearing before a judge, or a judge and a jury, to decide issues that are in conflict.

UNCONTESTED DIVORCE—a case in which both parties mutually agree to the divorce.

VERIFICATION—confirmation by affidavit or oath of the facts in the pleadings.

VISITATION—the right of the parent who does not have physical custody to visit his/her child, or have the child visit him/her.

VENUE—the county or city within the state that has the power to hear the case.

WAIVER—giving up a legal right, such as the right to alimony.

WITNESS—a person who testifies in court under oath to some fact that s/he knows. A witness may be a relative, neighbor, or co-worker, but the witness must know you and your spouse and have had enough contact with you to be able to swear in court that you have been separated from each other for the amount of time you stated in your Bill of Complaint for divorce.

Maryland Circuit & District Courts

Where to File Your Documents and Pay Filing Fees

All family law case documents are filed in a Circuit Court. The notable exception is a Petition For Protection From Domestic Violence—it can be filed in either a Circuit Court or a District Court. There are Circuit Courts and District Courts in all counties of the State.

Fees vary depending on the action, but in most cases the cost of a divorce action will be at least $90 plus a Master's Fee of approximately $110. The Master's Fee is often paid in advance at the same time that you file your complaint. Ask the clerk to tell you the amount of all fees and when they will need to be paid.

How to Ask to Delay or Excuse the Fees

To ask the court to delay or excuse the fees because you have little or no money or income, file Form Dom. Rel. 32 at the beginning of your case.

CIRCUIT COURTS IN MARYLAND

Allegany County
Circuit Court for Allegany County
P.O. Box 359
Washington Street
Cumberland, MD 21502 (301) 777-5922

Anne Arundel County
Circuit Court for Anne Arundel County
P. O. Box 71
Courthouse, Church Circle
Annapolis, MD 21404 (410) 222-1397

Baltimore City
Circuit Court for Baltimore City
111 North Calvert Street
Baltimore, MD 21202 (410) 333-3733

Baltimore County
Circuit Court for Baltimore County
P.O. Box 6754
County Courts Building, 401 Bosley Avenue
Towson, MD 21204 (410) 455-5066

Calvert County
Circuit Court for Calvert County
175 Main Street
Prince Frederick, MD 20678 (410) 535-1660

Caroline County
Circuit Court for Caroline County
Court House
Denton, MD 21629 (410) 479-1811

Carroll County
Circuit Court for Carroll County
P.O. Box 190
Westminster, MD 21157-0190 (410) 857-2026

Cecil County
Circuit Court for Cecil County
Court House, 129 East Main Street
Elkton, MD 21921 (410) 996-5373

Charles County
Circuit Court for Charles County
P.O. Box 3060
La Plata, MD 20646 (301) 932-3202

Dorchester County
Circuit Court for Dorchester County
P.O. Box 150
Courthouse
Cambridge, MD 21613 (410) 228-0481

Frederick County
Circuit Court for Frederick County
Court House, 100 West Patrick Street
Frederick, MD 21701 (301) 694-1976

Garrett County
Circuit Court for Garrett County
Court House
Oakland, MD 21550 (301) 334-1937

Harford County
Circuit Court for Harford County
Court House, 20 West Courtland Street
Bel Air, MD 21014 (410) 638-3426

Howard County
Circuit Court for Howard County
8360 Court Avenue
Ellicott City, MD 21043 (410) 313-2111

Kent County
Circuit Court for Kent County
Court House, 103 N. Cross Street
Chestertown, MD 21620 (410) 778-7460

Montgomery County
Circuit Court for Montgomery County
Montgomery County Judicial Center
50 Courthouse Square
Rockville, MD 20850 (301) 217-7202

Prince George's County
Circuit Court for Prince George's County
Court House
Upper Marlboro, MD 20772 (301) 952-3318

Queen Anne's County
Circuit Court for Queen Anne's County
Court House
Centreville, MD 21617 (410) 758-1773

St. Mary's County
Circuit Court for St. Mary's County
Court House
Leonardtown, MD 20650 (301) 475-4567

Somerset County
Circuit Court for Somerset County
Court House
Princess Anne, MD 21853 (410) 651-1555

Talbot County
Circuit Court for Talbot County
Court House
Easton, MD 21601 (410) 822-2611

Washington County
Circuit Court for Washington County
Court House
Hagerstown, MD 21740 (301) 733-8660

Wicomico County
Circuit Court for Wicomico County
Court House
Salisbury, MD 21801 (410) 543-6551

Worcester County
Circuit Court for Worcester County
P.O. Box 40
Court House, One West Market Street
Snow Hill, MD 21863-0040 (410) 632-1221

DISTRICT COURTS IN MARYLAND

Allegany County District Court: County Office Building, Cumberland. MD

Anne Arundel County: District Court, Annapolis, MD
     and District Court, Glen Burnie, MD

Baltimore City: District Court, Baltimore, MD

Baltimore County: District Court, Towson, MD

Calvert County: District Court, Prince Frederick, MD

Caroline County: District Court, Denton, MD

Carroll County: District Court, Westminster, MD

Cecil County: District Court, Elkton, MD

Charles County District Court: Courthouse, La Plata, MD

Dorchester County District Court: County Office Building Cambridge, MD

Frederick County: District Court, Frederick, MD

Garrett County: District Court, Oakland, MD

Harford County: District Court, Bel Air, MD

Howard County: District Court, Ellicott City, MD

Kent County: District Court, Chestertown, MD

Montgomery County: District Court, Rockville, MD
     and District Court, Silver Spring, MD

Prince George's County District Court: Courthouse, Upper Marlboro, MD
     and County Service Building, Hyattsville, MD

Queen Anne's County: District Court, Centreville, MD

St. Mary's County: District Court, Leonardtown, MD

Somerset County: District Court, Princess Anne, MD

Talbot County: District Court, Easton, MD

Washington County: District Court, Hagerstown, MD

Wicomico County: District Court, Salisbury, MD

Worcester County: District Court, Snowhill, MD

How To Do Your Own Divorce

This section of the book provides you with instructions and all the forms you need to file, as a *pro se* litigant, any of the major domestic relations actions related to the divorce process in a Maryland Circuit Court. (Other family law actions, such as guardianship and adoption, are not included because there are no Court-approved *pro se* forms available for them; therefore, these actions are beyond the scope of this book.)

How to Use This Section of the Book

The forms included in this section are copies of the Domestic Relations *Pro Se* Forms, often called the Dom. Rel. forms. The instructions, with some modifications, are also based on instructions that were released with the forms by the Administrative Office of the Courts, State of Maryland. These forms are the result of a special Task Force that was convened by the Maryland court system in 1994 to design a set of forms, with supporting instructions, that would be easy to use by *pro se* litigants. These forms have been in use since early 1995, and many thousands of individuals have used them successfully to file their own domestic actions. You can use these forms to file either a contested or uncontested action.

The Domestic Relations Pro Se *Forms*

As discussed in Part 1 of this book, it is not wise to try and represent yourself in a contested action. You should consult with and be represented by an attorney. Although the forms look simple to complete, representing yourself in a contested matter is very complex. In order to be effective you have to know the rules of evidence and understand other procedural rules that govern hearings before a Master or a Judge. Nevertheless, some persons have used these forms to initiate and represent themselves in contested cases.

All the domestic *pro se* forms are printed in numerical order in the last section of this book. As a first step you should copy and make a master set of all the forms. Then, make copies from the master set, and keep the master set filed away in a safe place for later possible use.

Copy the Pro Se *Forms*

You can also secure a copy of these forms and instructions from the Clerk's Office in any Circuit Court in Maryland. They are free. And the forms are also available on the Internet at the following Web sites: http://www.peoples-law.com at The People's Law Library of Maryland, and http://www.divorcelawinfo.com at the Divorce Law Information Service Center.

Forms Obtained from the Clerk, If Needed: DCI Report, "Blue Form," Child Support Guidelines Worksheet, and Differentiated Case Management Form

In some cases you may need several other forms to complete your action. These include the *Civil–Domestic Case Information (DCI) Report.* This Report helps the court determine how to schedule your case. Ask the Clerk if you need to file this form. If so, complete the form, checking each box that applies to your case and how your case should be scheduled.

Also obtained from the Clerk and called for in certain actions are the *Child Support Guidelines Worksheet* and the *"Blue Form,"* (*Maryland State Department of Health and Mental Hygiene: Report of Absolute Divorce or Annulment of Marriage*), which officially notifies the State of your separation or divorce.

Finally, the largest jurisdictions in Maryland (including Baltimore City, Montgomery County, Anne Arundel County, Prince George's County, and Baltimore County) have established the Differentiated Case Management System. This means that *if your case is uncontested, it will be assigned on a fast track for resolution.* When you file your complaint you must attach a Differentiated Case Management Form to the package. You get this form from the Clerk's Office in the county where you file your complaint.

Instructions That Accompany the Forms

Following this section of background material are the instructions: First read the General Instructions, and then read the Step-by-Step Instructions that apply to the action you wish to initiate. Next, match the forms with the instructions for your action and follow them exactly to pursue your case.

Variations Exist from County to County

The instructions that accompany these forms have *not* been modified for slight variations in local practice. In the State of Maryland, procedures are supposed to be uniform throughout the State. The reality is that there are slight variations in local practice that you have to follow in order to process your action as quickly and efficiently as possible. Check with the Clerk's Office in the Circuit Court where you are filing your action in order to make sure that you are in compliance with local practice.

On the Internet, you can access the People's Law Library of Maryland Web site, which contains more specific instructions for each of the major counties in Maryland and for each of the major actions. Also, The Divorce Law Information Service Center offers a low-cost information service that answers general legal questions for a modest fee. The Center also maintains a discussion group Maryland for *pro se* litigants. (See page 123)

Filing Fees and Master's Fees

Usually, there is a fee payable for each Complaint, Motion or Petition you file and a Master's Fee due for its subsequent hearing. These fees vary both with the type of action filed and from county to county in the State. The Filing Fee for a Complaint for Divorce is about $75, and the Master's Fee for a Divorce Hearing is about $125 (a total of about $200). The filing and Master's fees for other type actions, e.g., Petitions for Contempt and Modification, are about $25 and $50, respectively (about $75 total). The Master's Fee is often paid in advance at the same time that you file your complaint. *Ask the Clerk to tell you the amount of all fees and when they will need to be paid.*

Waiver of Fees

The *Motion for Waiver of Prepayment of Filing Fees and Other Court Costs,* Dom. Rel. 32, is meant only for those people who cannot afford to pay the court fees. (To check your eligibility and for instructions on how to file your request for the waiver of fees, see Page 93.)

General Instructions

First, read the preceding section; then these general instructions; and, finally, read the step-by-step instructions in the following section for the specific action you are filing. Next, make a copy of the forms that you need for the action that you are filing. You can complete these forms in pen *(but not pencil)*; they do not have to be typed.

Introduction

Generally, the initial filing requires either 1) a Complaint, Petition, or Motion (one of the Dom. Rel. forms); 2) a Civil–Domestic Case Information (DCI) Report; and 3) a Financial Statement (if custody, child support, alimony, or a waiver of fees is involved). If you intend to file a *Motion for Waiver of Prepayment of Fees and Other Court Costs, Dom. Rel. 1 00*, you will have to have completed that also on/or before the initial filing.

1. Complete the Forms

Usually, you will need to make at least 3 copies of the completed forms: one for your records and an additional copy for each opposing party. An example of the need for multiple copies for opposing parties is when filing a *Petition/Motion to Modify Child Support*, you may need one copy for the other parent of the child and another for the local child support enforcement agency in your area where you pay your child support.

2. Make Copies

All family law cases are filed in a Circuit Court. (A *Petition for Protection From Domestic Violence*, however, can be filed in either a Circuit Court or District Court.) There are Circuit Courts and District Courts in all counties of the State. If you are filing a Complaint, Petition, or Motion for a divorce case, it must be filed in the county where you live or where the other side lives or works. For a case about custody, visitation, or child support it can generally be filed where the child or either parent lives. If there is an earlier case between you and your (ex-)spouse in one county, you may not be able to file this case in a different county.

3. Where to File Your Forms

File the *original* copy of your completed forms. At this time you will have to pay the filing fee and in some jurisdictions you will also pay the Master's fee. If your jurisdiction does not require you to pay the Master's fee at this time, you may be required to pay later. If you are requesting the Waiver of

4. File Your Forms and Pay Fees

Fees, you must file that Motion along with your forms now. (Unless you have already filed and been granted the Waiver of fees—then file the granted Waiver at this time.) If you are going to use the Sheriff to do service, you should let the clerk know when you file. Also, ask the Clerk for your Case Number, and write it down.

5. Wait   Do not attempt to serve the other side until you have a case number and a *Writ of Summons*. The court will issue a Summons that will be sent to your home in 5–10 days. You should receive an original and 2 copies of this form; if you do not, then make copies (original copy–service package; 1 copy–your records; 1 copy–attach to Affidavit of Service). The Summons is mailed to you, but the letter inside is addressed to the opposing party. It tells the other party how long (30–90 days) s/he has to answer your Complaint or Petition/Motion in writing. A 30-day Summons is for someone who will be served in the State of Maryland. A 60-day Summons is for someone who will be served in one of the other states. A 90-day Summons is for someone who will be served in another country. Check your summons to be sure that it has the correct designation for your situation.

6. Service   Service is the legal way that the other party receives (is served) the original Summons and one copy of the forms that you filed with the court. All papers you file with the court must also be served on the other side. If you are starting a case, your case cannot go forward until the other side is served.

Personal Service of your Complaint is the preferred method—this means hand delivery of the Summons and documents to the other party by either the Sheriff, a Process Server, or a personal friend. Postal delivery via Certified Mail–Restricted Delivery–Return Receipt Requested is acceptable, too.

Under no circumstances can you do service yourself; it must be done by someone else who is over the age of 18. It is very important that you do service correctly. If you do not, then the court may dismiss your case.

If you have a *domestic violence situation* and you are concerned for your safety, you should have an attorney. S/he would be able to help keep your whereabouts secret.

The only ways to obviate service are: if the opposing party files his/her Answer (submits to the jurisdiction of the court); if the opposing party joins you on a consent order (usually associated with a custody case); or if an attorney makes a motion to waive service and the court grants that motion (almost never granted).

7. Return of Service   If service is to be done by a Sheriff in Maryland, the Clerk will send the Summons and Complaint directly to the Sheriff. The Sheriff will return the *Affidavit of Service* and *Writ of Summons* directly to the Clerk for filing. You should call the Clerk's office to make sure when service has been completed.

If you have not used the Sheriff to do service, then you must file the appropriate Affidavit of Service, either Dom. Rel. 55 or Dom. Rel. 56. This form is filled out by the person who has done service for you. It should be filed along with a copy of the Summons to show that you have done service within the appropriate amount of time.

If service was done by *personal service*, have the friend or process server who served the defendant complete Affidavit, Dom. Rel. 55, and return it to you for filing with the Clerk. Attach a copy of the Summons.

If service was by certified mail, return the Affidavit, Dom. Rel. 56, with the Return Receipt (green card) attached and file with the Clerk. Attach a copy of the Summons.

The other party has a set number of days to answer in writing: 30 days to answer if s/he is served in Maryland, 60 days to answer if s/he is served out of state, and 90 days to answer if s/he is served outside of the United States. When that period has ended, you can call the Clerk's Office to see if an Answer has been filed. If no Answer has been filed, you may file the *Request for Order of Default,* Dom. Rel. 54.

8. The Other Party Has Time to Answer

If you have completed service correctly, and the other party has not filed an Answer by the appropriate time, you can file a *Request for Order of Default,* Dom. Rel. 54. This form asks the court to take action in the event the other party does not show up at the hearing. You will receive a signed copy of the Order of Default in the mail. (If service was not done correctly, your Request for Order of Default will be denied.)

9. Request for Order of Default if No Answer is Filed

There may have to be several attempts to serve the other side, and these may require using different methods. A *Writ of Summons* is only good for 60 days. If the other side has not been served within 60 days, you will have to ask the Clerk of Court in writing to issue a new Summons.

10. What Happens If Service Is Not Made in Time?

In some jurisdictions, the Return of Service will trigger the docket and set your hearing or conference date. Other jurisdictions require that you file a *Request for Master's Hearing,* Dom. Rel. 51, or a *Request for Trial on the Merit,* Dom. Rel. 52. (Ask your Clerk for guidance at the time that you file your Return of Service.) The court will notify you by mail of the date, time, and place for your hearing or of the steps you need to follow to set up a hearing with a Master Examiner for an uncontested divorce. To ensure that you get all notices and papers in your case, make sure the Clerk of Court and the other side always have your correct address. Immediately notify the Clerk and the other side in writing if you move.

11. Requesting Your Hearing

On the day your case is scheduled, make sure that you arrive there early. Often you will need to check in with the court personnel in the courtroom. If you are not there when your case is called, your case could be thrown out or the court could rule in favor of the other side. If you have to miss your court date because of an emergency, call the court before you are scheduled to be in court. The kind of hearing you will have will vary depending on the kind of action you have filed. The specific instructions for each action list any special requirements for the hearing for that action.

12. The Hearing

Step-by-Step Instructions

Follow the step-by-step instructions to complete the forms. For further help and information refer back to the preceding two sections.

INSTRUCTIONS FOR FILING
MOTION FOR WAIVER OF PREPAYMENT OF FILING FEES AND OTHER COURT COSTS
Dom. Rel. 32

The *Motion for Waiver of Prepayment of Fees* is meant only for those people who cannot afford to pay the court fees.

COMPLETE 4 Steps to File This Motion.

STEP 1 —Check Your Eligibility.

To see if you qualify for the waiver: find your family size, and read across the same line. If your income is less than the amount shown, you qualify.

Family Size	Annual Income	Monthly Income	Weekly Income
1 person	$13,966/year	$1,164/month	$269/week
2 persons	$18,264/year	$1,522/month	$351/week
3 persons	$22,561/year	$1,522/month	$434/week
4 persons	$26,859/year	$1,880/month	$517/week
5 persons	$31,156/year	$2,238/month	$599/week
6 persons	$35,454/year	$2,596/month	$682/week
7 persons	$36,260/year	$2,954/month	$697/week
8 persons	$37,065/year	$3,089/month	$713/week
9 persons	$37,870/year	$3,156/month	$728/week
10 persons	$38,677/year	$3,223/month	$744/week

STEP 2 —Complete the Following Forms:
Dom. Rel. 32, Motion for Waiver of Prepayment of Fees
Dom. Rel. 31, Financial Statement (Long Form)
You should request waiver of all filing fees, court costs, and the Master's Fee.

STEP 3 —Make Copies.
Make 3 copies of the Motion and Financial Statement.

STEP 4 —File Forms.
File the original copies of the above forms (Motion and Financial Statement) with the Clerk of Court where you live.

When to File Your Request   In some Circuit Courts you must file your request for a Waiver of fees *before* you initially file your Petition or Complaint; in other jurisdictions you file this request along with your Petition or Complaint. Check first with the Clerk of Court in your area for the proper time to file your request for a waiver of fees.

The Clerk will deliver your Motion for waiver of fees to the Administrative Judge, who will either approve or reject your Motion. Five days after filing your request call the Clerk to find out if your Waiver of fees has been granted.

If your Motion is granted, you will not have to pay fees at the time you file your Petition/Motion or Complaint. The approval means that the fees are deferred or waived. Under some circumstances, the Master in a final hearing, or the Judge at a trial, could decide that you are responsible for paying court fees and will direct you to pay them; however, this is unlikely.

INSTRUCTIONS FOR SERVICE
Dom. Rel. 55 or Dom. Rel. 56

Service is the legal way that the other party, your (ex-)spouse, gets the original Summons and one copy of all the forms that you filed with the court. If you are starting a case, your case cannot go forward until the other side is served.

Under no circumstances can you do service yourself; it must be done by someone else over the age of 18. It is very important that you do service correctly. If you do not, then the court may dismiss your case.

After you file your Petition/Motion or Complaint, the court will issue a *Writ of Summons* which will be sent to your home in 5–10 days. Do not attempt to serve the other side until you have a Case Number and a Summons. You should receive an original and 2 copies of the Summons; if you do not, then make copies (the original Summons goes in your Service Package; 1 copy is for your records; and (later) 1 copy will be attached to the Affidavit of Service).

STEP 1 —**Put Together Your Service Package:**
Attach the original copy of the Summons to one copy of *all of the forms* that you filed with the court for your Petition/Motion or Complaint.

STEP 2 —**Choose One of the Following Methods of Service:**
Personal Service is the preferred method of service—this means you use the Sheriff, a Process Server, or a friend to hand deliver the summons. If you don't use personal service, you must use Certified Mail to deliver the summons.

Sheriff. The Sheriff's office will deliver the service package and complete the Affidavit for a fee of around $30–$40. The Sheriff will return the Affidavit of Service and Writ of Summons directly to the Clerk for filing.

Private Process by a Process Server. You can check in your phone book or with any local attorney to find a process server. For a fee this person will deliver the service package for you. You must get them to complete an *Affidavit of Service* (Private Process, Dom. Rel. 55). Then, you file the Affidavit with a copy of the Summons attached at the Civil Desk of the Circuit Court.

Private Process by a Friend. Any adult over the age of 18, *but not you,* may hand deliver the service package to the opposing party. They may *not* leave the package on their doorstep, or with a roommate, or with a relative. The service package must be put in their hand. You must get that friend to complete an *Affidavit of Service* (Private Process, Dom. Rel. 55). Then you file the Affidavit along with a copy of the Summons at the Civil Desk of the Circuit Court.

Certified Mail, Restricted Delivery, Return Receipt Requested. Any adult over the age of 18, *but not you,* may take the service package to the post office to mail it in the above manner. Then that person must fill out an *Affidavit of Service* (Dom. Rel. 56, Certified Mail). When the post office returns the green card (this card is the Return Receipt you requested), check the signature on it. If the signature is not by the person you sent it to, service has not been completed—try again. If the signature is correct, attach the green card and a copy of the Summons to the Affidavit of Service, Dom. Rel. 56, and file it at the Civil Desk of the Circuit Court.

COMPLAINT FOR CHILD SUPPORT
(Dom. Rel. 1)

If there is no Court Order for support of a child in your care, you may initiate a case to obtain support of that child from the parent(s)/other parent, filing either through an attorney, through your local child support enforcement office, or by yourself. You should consider using the child support enforcement agency in the county where you live. They will assign an attorney to your case, for a very small fee, to represent you only for child support in a child support action.

If you cannot afford court fees, you may be eligible for the Waiver of Fees (see instructions on page 93).

COMPLETE 8 steps to proceed with the case yourself.

STEP 1 —Complete the Following Forms:
Civil–Domestic Case Information (DCI) Report (if needed)
Dom. Rel. 1: Complaint for Child Support
Dom. Rel. 30: Financial Statement (Child Support)
Earnings Withholding Order (if you are requesting Wage Withholding)

STEP 2 —Make Copies.
Make 3 copies of the DCI Report, Complaint, Financial Statement, and Withholding Order

STEP 3 —File your Forms and Pay the Filing Fee.
File the original copies of the above forms at the Civil Desk of the Circuit Court where you live (DCI Report, Complaint, Financial Statement, and Withholding Order, if used). Don't forget to sign and date the forms.

A filing fee and sometimes a Master's fee are required at this time. If you are requesting the Waiver of Fees, you must file that Motion along with your forms now. (If you have already filed and been granted the Waiver of fees—then file the granted Waiver at this time in order to avoid paying the fees.)

If you plan to serve the other party out of state, ask the Clerk for a *Writ of Summons* for 60 days. If you plan to serve the other party outside the United States, ask the Clerk for a 90-day Writ of Summons.

STEP 4 —Service.
Follow instructions on Page 94.
You must serve the other party correctly after you file your Complaint and receive your Writ of Summons, or your case cannot go forward.

STEP 5 —Return Completed Affidavit of Service, Dom. Rel. 55 or 56.
Have the person who served the defendant complete Dom. Rel. 55 and return it to you for filing with the Clerk. If service was by Certified Mail you complete and return Dom. Rel. 56.

If service was done by a Sheriff in Maryland, the Clerk will have sent the Summons and Complaint directly to the Sheriff. And the Sheriff will return the Affidavit of Service and Writ of Summons directly to the Clerk for filing.

STEP 6 —**Request for Order of Default if No Answer is Filed**

If your (ex-)spouse is served in Maryland, s/he must answer within 30 days .

If your (ex-)spouse is served in another state, s/he must answer within 60 days.

If your (ex-)spouse is served in another country, s/he must answer within 90 days.

If your (ex-)spouse has not filed an Answer by the appropriate time, complete and file a *Request for Order of Default,* Dom. Rel. 54. (Follow step-by-step instructions on page 120.) You will receive a signed copy of the granted Order of Default in the mail.

STEP 7 —**Request for Master's Hearing or Trial on the Merits.**

After you have received either an Answer or an Order of Default, file a *Request for Master's Hearing*, Dom. Rel. 51, or a *Request for Trial on the Merits,* Dom. Rel. 52, so that a court date will be set. In some counties you will not have to file a Request for a Master's Hearing; you simply contact the Master directly and set up a date for the hearing. The Master's fee will vary from county to county in Maryland.

STEP 8 —**Prepare for the Hearing.**

Whether or not the other party has answered, send him/her a notice of the date, time, and place of the hearing and either file a copy of the notice with the Court or bring a copy to the hearing. Request subpoenas from the Clerk for any witnesses or documents needed at the hearing.

You must bring a completed *Child Support Guidelines Worksheet* to the hearing or trial. You will have to show your income and expenses and those of the defendant. You can secure a Child Support Guidelines Worksheet from the Clerk of Court.

If you have access to the Internet, you can test your calculations, by using the Child Support Calculators that are at http://www.peoples-law.com located in the Family Law Center of the The People's Law Library of Maryland. If you are unable to do this, you may want to see an attorney or go to your local child support enforcement office.

Hearing Checklist. When you come to court you should have:

✓__Your Child Support Guidelines Worksheet

✓__Your last three pay stubs

✓__Your last two tax returns

PETITION FOR CONTEMPT:
FAILURE TO PAY CHILD SUPPORT
(Dom. Rel. 2)

If a parent of your child(ren) or a parent of a child(ren) in your care has been ordered by a court to pay child support and is not paying, you may ask the court to enforce its order, filing either through an attorney, through your local child support enforcement office, or by yourself. You should consider using the child support enforcement agency in the county where you live. They will assign an attorney to your case, for a very small fee, to represent you only for child support in a child support action.

Use this form *only* if you already have a Court Order for payment. To complete this form you will need a copy of that Order. If you do not have a copy, ask the Clerk of Court how to get one.

If you cannot afford court fees, you may be eligible for the Waiver of Fees (see instructions on page 93).

COMPLETE 8 steps to proceed with the case yourself.

STEP 1 —Complete the Following Forms:
> Civil–Domestic Case Information (DCI) Report (if needed)
> Dom. Rel. 2: Petition for Contempt
> Dom. Rel. 30: Financial Statement (Child Support)
> Dom. Rel. 53: Show Cause Order

To complete Line 2 of Dom. Rel. 2—refer back to the Court Order for the date, the city or county where the Order was granted, the case number, the name of the person ordered to pay, and the amount he/she was ordered to pay. Then, circle whether the payments were to be made weekly, bimonthly or monthly.

Note that on Line 5 of Dom. Rel. 2 you need to circle whether you do or do not want the court to order jail time to enforce its Order.

Fill in only the top of the Show Cause Order (Dom. Rel. 53) and attach it to the Petition (Dom. Rel. 2).

STEP 2 —Make Copies.
Make 3 copies of the DCI Report, Petition, Show Cause Order, and Financial Statement.

STEP 3 —File your Forms and Pay the Filing Fee.
File the original copies of the above forms at the Civil Desk of the Circuit Court where you live (DCI Report, Petition, Show Cause Order, and Financial Statement). Don't forget to sign and date the forms.

A filing fee and sometimes a Master's fee are required at this time. If you are requesting the Waiver of Fees, you must file that Motion along with your forms now. (If you have already filed and been granted the Waiver of fees—then file the granted Waiver at this time in order to avoid paying the fees.)

If you plan to serve the other party out of state, ask the Clerk for a 60-day *Writ of Summons*. If you plan to serve the other party out of the country, ask the Clerk for a 90-day *Writ of Summons*.

STEP 4 —Service.

Follow instructions on Page 94.
You must serve the other party correctly after you file your Petition and receive your Writ of Summons, or your case cannot go forward.

STEP 5 —Return Completed Affidavit of Service, Dom. Rel. 55 or 56.

Have the person who served the defendant complete Dom. Rel. 55 and return it to you for filing with the Clerk. If service was by Certified Mail you complete and return Dom. Rel. 56.

If service was done by a Sheriff in Maryland, the Clerk will have sent the Summons and Petition directly to the Sheriff. And the Sheriff will return the Affidavit of Service and Writ of Summons directly to the Clerk for filing.

STEP 6 —Request for Default if No Answer is Filed.

If your (ex-)spouse is served in Maryland, s/he must answer within 30 days. If your (ex-)spouse is served in another state, s/he must answer within 60 days. If your (ex-)spouse is served in another country, s/he must answer within 90 days.

If your (ex-)spouse has not filed an Answer by the appropriate time, complete and file a *Request for Order of Default,* Dom. Rel. 54. (Follow step-by-step instructions on page 120.) You will receive a signed copy of the granted Order of Default in the mail.

STEP 7 —Request for Master's Hearing or Trial on the Merits

After you have received either an Answer or an Order of Default, file a *Request for Master's Hearing*, Dom. Rel. 51, or a *Request for Trial on the Merits*, Dom. Rel. 52, so that a court date will be set. In some counties you will not have to file a *Request for a Master's Hearing*; you simply contact the Master directly and set up a date for the hearing. The Master's fee will vary from county to county in Maryland.

STEP 8 —Prepare for the Hearing.

If the court signs the Show Cause Order, a copy of it will be mailed back to you. The court will have filled in the court date. Whether or not the other party answered, send him/her a notice of the date, time, and place of the hearing and either file a copy of the notice with the Court or bring a copy to the hearing.

PETITION FOR CONTEMPT:
DENIAL OF VISITATION
(Dom. Rel. 3)

If you have a Court Order granting you visitation and the person with custody has denied you visitation, you may ask the court to enforce its Order so that you can see the child(ren), filing either through an attorney or by yourself.

Use this form *only* if there is already a Court Order that allows you visitation. To complete this form you will need a copy of that Order. If you do not have a copy, ask the Clerk of Court how to get one.

If you cannot afford to pay the filing fees for this action, you may be eligible for the Waiver of Fees (see instructions on page 93).

Complete 8 steps to proceed with the case yourself.

STEP 1 —Complete the Following Forms:
Civil–Domestic Case Information (DCI) Report (if needed)
Dom. Rel. 3: Petition for Contempt
Dom. Rel. 53: Show Cause Order

To complete Line 1 of Dom. Rel. 3—refer back to the Court Order for the date, the city or county where the Order was granted, and the case number.

Note that on Line 2 of Dom. Rel. 3, you must explain to the court in detail the dates and events surrounding the denial of your visitation.

On Line 5 of Dom. Rel. 3, you need to circle whether you do or do not want the court to order jail time to enforce its Order.

In the section titled, *FOR THESE REASONS*, fill in the name of the person with custody. Then state what you would like the court to do in addition to what is listed, if anything, but remember that the court need not give you what you ask for.

Fill in only the top of the Show Cause Order (Dom. Rel. 53) and attach it to the Petition (Dom. Rel. 2).

STEP 2 —Make Copies.
Make 3 copies of the DCI Report, Petition, and Show Cause Order

STEP 3 —File your Forms and Pay the Filing Fee.
File the original copies of the above forms at the Civil Desk of the Circuit Court where you live (DCI Report, Petition, and Show Cause Order). Don't forget to sign and date the forms.

A filing fee and sometimes a Master's fee are required at this time. If you are requesting the Waiver of Fees, you must file that Motion along with your forms now. (If you have already filed and been granted the Waiver of fees—then file the granted Waiver at this time in order to avoid paying the fees.)

If you plan to serve the other party out of state, ask the Clerk for a 60-day *Writ of Summons*. If you plan to serve the other party out of the country, ask the Clerk for a 90-day Writ of Summons.

STEP 4 —Service.

Follow instructions on Page 94.
You must serve the other party correctly after you file your Petition and receive your Writ of Summons, or your case cannot go forward.

STEP 5 —Return Completed Affidavit of Service, Dom. Rel. 55 or 56.

Have the person who served the defendant complete Dom. Rel. 55 and return it to you for filing with the Clerk. If service was by Certified Mail you complete and return Dom. Rel. 56.

If service was done by a Sheriff in Maryland, the Clerk will have sent the Summons and Petition directly to the Sheriff. And the Sheriff will return the Affidavit of Service and Writ of Summons directly to the Clerk for filing.

STEP 6 —Request for Default if No Answer is Filed.

If your (ex-)spouse is served in Maryland, s/he must answer within 30 days. If your (ex-)spouse is served in another state, s/he must answer within 60 days. If your (ex-)spouse is served in another country, s/he must answer within 90 days.

If your (ex-)spouse has not filed an Answer by the appropriate time, complete and file a *Request for Order of Default,* Dom. Rel. 54. (Follow step-by-step instructions on page 120.) You will receive a signed copy of the granted Order of Default in the mail.

STEP 7 —Request for Master's Hearing or Trial on the Merits.

After you have received either an Answer or an Order of Default, file a *Request for Master's Hearing*, Dom. Rel. 51, or a *Request for Trial on the Merits*, Dom. Rel. 52, so that a court date will be set. In some counties you will not have to file a *Request for a Master's Hearing*; you simply contact the Master directly and set up a date for the hearing. The Master's fee will vary from county to county in Maryland.

STEP 8 —Prepare for the Hearing.

If the court signs the Show Cause Order, a copy of it will be mailed back to you. The court will have filled in the court date. Whether or not the other party answered, send him/her a notice of the date, time, and place of the hearing and either file a copy of the notice with the Court or bring a copy to the hearing.

COMPLAINT FOR CUSTODY
(Dom. Rel. 4)

If there is no Court Order granting custody of a child, you may initiate a case to obtain custody of that child, filing either through an attorney or by yourself.

Custody, *if contested*, is one of the most difficult types of cases, and you should seriously consider using an attorney, rather than representing yourself.

If you cannot afford to pay the filing fees for this action, you may be eligible for the Waiver of Fees (see instructions on page 93).

Complete 8 steps to proceed with the case yourself.

STEP 1 —Complete the Following Forms:
Civil–Domestic Case Information (DCI) Report (if needed)
Dom. Rel. 4: Complaint for Custody
Dom. Rel. 30: Financial Statement (Child Support)

On Dom. Rel. 4, do not write anything in where it says "Case No." The Clerk of Court will fill in this blank and, at that time, you should make note of the number for future reference.

On Dom. Rel. 4, if you are not a parent (e.g., grandparent), fill in the name of one parent as "Defendant No. 1," and the other parent as "Defendant No. 2."

On Dom. Rel. 4, list the current address and telephone number for each defendant.

On Dom. Rel. 4, in the section titled, *FOR THESE REASONS*, check off everything you want—but remember the court need not give you what you ask for.

Visitation: You can ask the court to allow the Defendant(s) unrestricted visitation with the children; to allow the Defendant(s) visitation on a certain schedule or with supervision; or to bar visitation by the Defendant(s). You should have a good reason for asking to bar visitation, and the reason(s) should be stated after the word "because."

Health Insurance: You can ask the court to order the parent(s)/other parent to include the child(ren) on his/her/their health insurance.

Child Support: You can ask the court to order the parent(s)/other parent to pay child support. If you want child support, you should complete a financial statement (Dom. Rel. 30 or 31) and file it with form Dom. Rel. 4.

Other Requests: If you wish the court to order anything else that relates to the child(ren), you should list it here.

STEP 2 —Make Copies.
Make 3 copies of the DCI Report, Complaint, and Financial Statement.

STEP 3 —File your Forms and Pay the Filing Fee.
File the original copies of the above forms at the Civil Desk of the Circuit Court where you live (DCI Report, Complaint, and Financial Statement). Don't forget to sign and date the forms.

A filing fee and sometimes a Master's fee are required at this time. If you are requesting the Waiver of Fees, you must file that Motion along with your forms now. (If you have already filed and been granted the Waiver of fees—then file the granted Waiver at this time in order to avoid paying the fees.)

If you plan to serve the other party out of state, ask the Clerk for a 60-day *Writ of Summons*. If you plan to serve the other party out of the country, ask the Clerk for a 90-day Writ of Summons.

STEP 4 —Service.

Follow instructions on Page 94.

You must serve the other party correctly after you file your Complaint and receive your Writ of Summons, or your case cannot go forward.

STEP 5 —Return Completed Affidavit of Service, Dom. Rel. 55 or 56.

Have the person who served the defendant complete Dom. Rel. 55 and return it to you for filing with the Clerk. If service was by Certified Mail you complete and return Dom. Rel. 56.

If service was done by a Sheriff in Maryland, the Clerk will have sent the Summons and Complaint directly to the Sheriff. And the Sheriff will return the Affidavit of Service and Writ of Summons directly to the Clerk for filing.

STEP 6 —Request for Default if No Answer is Filed.

If your (ex-)spouse is served in Maryland, s/he must answer within 30 days. If your (ex-)spouse is served in another state, s/he must answer within 60 days. If your (ex-)spouse is served in another country, s/he must answer within 90 days.

If your (ex-)spouse has not filed an Answer by the appropriate time, file a *Request for Order of Default,* Dom. Rel. 54. (See step-by-step instructions on page 120.) You will receive a signed copy of the granted Order of Default in the mail.

STEP 7 —Request for Master's Hearing or Trial on the Merits.

After you have received either an Answer or an Order of Default, file a *Request for Master's Hearing,* Dom. Rel. 51, or a *Request for Trial on the Merits,* Dom. Rel. 52, so that a court date will be set. In some counties you will not have to file a *Request for a Master's Hearing;* you simply contact the Master directly and set up a date for the hearing. The Master's fee will vary from county to county in Maryland.

STEP 8 —Prepare for the Hearing.

Whether or not the other party answered, send him/her a notice of the date, time, and place of the hearing and either file a copy of the notice with the Court or bring a copy to the hearing. If custody is contested, you will have to prove that it is in the best interests of the child that you have sole or joint custody. You may have to bring one or more expert witnesses who can testify to what is in the best interests of the child. It is very difficult to represent yourself in a contested custody matter.

COMPLAINT FOR VISITATION
(Dom. Rel. 5)

If there is no Court Order giving you visitation, you may: (1) obtain the services of an attorney to handle your case; or (2) file the case yourself by using this form.

Use this form *only* if there is no Order giving you visitation, and you are *only* seeking visitation. If there is an existing Order for visitation, you should use form Dom. Rel. 7: Petition/Motion to Modify Visitation.

If you cannot afford court fees, you may be eligible for the Waiver of Fees (see instructions on page 93).

Complete 8 steps to proceed with the case yourself.

STEP 1 —**Complete the Following Forms:**
Civil–Domestic Case Information (DCI) Report (if needed)
Dom. Rel. 5: Complaint for Visitation

On Dom. Rel. 5, list the current address and telephone number for each defendant. In the section titled, *FOR THESE REASONS*, explain how often, on what holidays, and where you want to be allowed to see the child(ren).

STEP 2 —**Make Copies.**
Make 3 copies of the DCI Report and Complaint.

STEP 3 — **File your Forms and Pay the Filing Fee.**
File the original copies of the above forms at the Civil Desk of the Circuit Court where you live (DCI Report and Complaint). Don't forget to sign and date the forms.

A filing fee and sometimes a Master's fee are required at this time. If you are requesting the Waiver of Fees, you must file that Motion along with your forms now. (If you have already filed and been granted the Waiver of fees—then file the granted Waiver at this time in order to avoid paying the fees.)

If you plan to serve the other party out of state, ask the Clerk for a 60-day *Writ of Summons*. If you plan to serve the other party out of the country, ask the Clerk for a 90-day *Writ of Summons*.

The Clerk will assign your action a case number—make sure you write it down.

STEP 4 —**Service.**
Follow instructions on Page 94.
You must serve the other party correctly after you file your Complaint and receive your Writ of Summons, or your case cannot go forward.

STEP 5 —**Return Completed Affidavit of Service, Dom. Rel. 55 or 56.**
Have the person who served the defendant complete Dom. Rel. 55 and return it to you for filing with the Clerk. If service was by Certified Mail you complete and return Dom. Rel. 56.

If service was done by a Sheriff in Maryland, the Clerk will have sent the Summons and Complaint directly to the Sheriff. And the Sheriff will return the Affidavit of Service and Writ of Summons directly to the Clerk for filing.

STEP 6 —Request for Default if No Answer is Filed.

If your (ex-)spouse is served in Maryland, s/he must answer within 30 days. If your (ex-)spouse is served in another state, s/he must answer within 60 days. If your (ex-)spouse is served in another country, s/he must answer within 90 days.

If your (ex-)spouse has not filed an Answer by the appropriate time, complete and file a *Request for Order of Default,* Dom. Rel. 54. (Follow step-by-step instructions on page 120.) You will receive a signed copy of the granted Order of Default in the mail.

STEP 7 —Request for Master's Hearing or Trial on the Merits.

After you have received either an Answer or an Order of Default, file a *Request for Master's Hearing,* Dom. Rel. 51, or a *Request for Trial on the Merits,* Dom. Rel. 52, so that a court date will be set. In some counties you will not have to file a *Request for a Master's Hearing;* you simply contact the Master directly and set up a date for the hearing. The Master's fee will vary depending on the county within Maryland.

STEP 8 —Prepare for the Hearing.

Whether or not the other party answered, send him/her a notice of the date, time, and place of the hearing and either file a copy of the notice with the Court or bring a copy to the hearing. In the hearing you should be prepared to prove that the visitation schedule that you propose is in the best interests of the child.

PETITION/MOTION TO MODIFY CHILD SUPPORT
(Dom. Rel. 6)

If you have a Court Order to pay or receive child support (for example, from a divorce or paternity decree), it may be possible to have the court modify the amount you are currently paying or receiving. There are three ways you can do this: (1) obtain the service of an attorney to handle your case; (2) go to the Bureau of Support Enforcement (BOSE) in your county; or (3) file the case yourself by using form Dom. Rel. 6.

Use this Petition/Motion *only* if there is an existing child support Order and you are *not* receiving public assistance or welfare. In order to complete this form you will need a copy of your existing child support Order. If you do not have a copy, ask the Clerk of Court how to get one.

If you cannot afford court fees, you may be eligible for the Waiver of Fees (see instructions on page 93).

Complete 8 steps to proceed with the case yourself.

STEP 1 —**Complete the Following forms:**
Civil–Domestic Case Information (DCI) Report (if needed)
Dom. Rel. 6: Petition/Motion to Modify Child Support
Dom. Rel. 30 or Dom. Rel. 31, Financial Statement (Child Support)

On Dom. Rel. 6, fill in the case number exactly as it appears on the child support Order and then copy the name(s) of the Plaintiff and Defendant(s) exactly as they appear on the Order. Then, fill in the date, city or county where the Order was granted, the case number, the name of the person with custody, and the name of the person(s) granted visitation.

On line 3 of Dom. Rel. 6, you must explain what change of circumstances justifies a change in child support. There must be a substantial change in circumstances. This is interpreted to mean that your income must either have either increased of decreased by 35% during the most recent time period.

STEP 2 —**Make Copies.**
Make 3 copies of the DCI Report, Petition/Motion, and Financial Statement.

STEP 3 —**File your Forms and Pay the Filing Fee.**
File the original copies of the above forms at the Civil Desk of the Circuit Court where you live (DCI Report, Petition/Motion, and Financial Statement) Don't forget to sign and date the forms.

A filing fee and sometimes a Master's fee are required at this time. If you are requesting the Waiver of Fees, you must file that Motion along with your forms now. (If you have already filed and been granted the Waiver of fees—then file the granted Waiver at this time in order to avoid paying the fees.)

If you plan to serve the other party out of state, ask the Clerk for a 60-day *Writ of Summons*. If you plan to serve the other party out of the country, ask the Clerk for a 90-day Writ of Summons.

STEP 4 —**Service.**

Follow instructions on Page 94.

You must serve the other party correctly after you file your Petition/Motion and receive your Writ of Summons, or your case cannot go forward.

STEP 5 —**Return Completed Affidavit of Service, Dom. Rel. 55 or 56.**

Have the person who served the defendant complete Dom. Rel. 55 and return it to you for filing with the Clerk. If service was by Certified Mail you complete and return Dom. Rel. 56.

If service was done by a Sheriff in Maryland, the Clerk will have sent the Summons and Petition directly to the Sheriff. And the Sheriff will return the Affidavit of Service and Writ of Summons directly to the Clerk for filing.

STEP 6 —**Request for Default if No Answer is Filed.**

If your (ex-)spouse is served in Maryland, s/he must answer within 30 days. If your (ex-)spouse is served in another state, s/he must answer within 60 days. If your (ex-)spouse is served in another country, s/he must answer within 90 days.

If your (ex-)spouse has not filed an Answer by the appropriate time, complete and file a *Request for Order of Default,* Dom. Rel. 54. (Follow step-by-step instructions on page 120.) You will receive a signed copy of the granted Order of Default in the mail.

STEP 7 —**Request for Master's Hearing or Trial on the Merits.**

After you have received either an Answer or an Order of Default, file a *Request for Master's Hearing,* Dom. Rel. 51, or a *Request for Trial on the Merits,* Dom. Rel. 52, so that a court date will be set. In some counties you will not have to file a *Request for a Master's Hearing*; you simply contact the Master directly and set up a date for the hearing. The Master's fee varies from county to county in Maryland.

STEP 8 —**Prepare for the Hearing.**

Whether or not the other party answered, send him/her a notice of the date, time, and place of the hearing and either file a copy of the notice with the Court or bring a copy to the hearing.

Hearing Checklist. When you come to court you should have:
✓__Completed Child Support Guidelines Worksheet [if requesting a change of custody]
✓__A copy of any previous child support Order
✓__Your last three pay stubs
✓__Your last two tax returns
✓__Any witnesses who may help the court to see why this change is best for your child(ren)

PETITION/MOTION TO MODIFY CUSTODY/VISITATION
(Dom. Rel. 7)

If you already have a Court Order for custody or visitation, you can request the court to change custody or visitation. To do this you may: (1) obtain the services of an attorney to handle your case; or (2) file the case yourself by using Dom. Rel. 7.

Use this form *only* if there is already a Court Order for custody or visitation and you were *named* as a Plaintiff or Defendant in that court case.

If you cannot afford court fees, you may be eligible for the Waiver of Fees (see instructions on page 93).

Complete 8 steps to proceed with the case yourself.

STEP 1 —Complete the Following Forms:
Civil—Domestic Case Information (DCI) Report (if needed)
Dom. Rel. 7: Petition/Motion to Modify Custody/Visitation
Dom. Rel. 30: Financial Statement (If requesting change in custody)

On Dom. Rel. 7, fill in the case number exactly as it appears on the Order for custody or visitation, and copy the name(s) of the Plaintiff and Defendant(s) exactly as they appear on the Order.

Then, fill in the date, city or county where the Order was granted, the case number, the name of the person with custody, and the name of the person(s) granted visitation.

On line 3 of Dom. Rel. 7, you must explain what change of circumstances justifies a change in the child custody or visitation arrangements. You must show that it is in the best interest of the child(ren) to make this change.

On Dom. Rel. 7, in the section titled, *FOR THESE REASONS*, you explain how you would like the custody/visitation to be changed.

STEP 2 —Make Copies.
Make 3 copies of the DCI Report, Petition/Motion, and Financial Statement.

STEP 3 —File your Forms and Pay the Filing Fee.
File the original copies of the above forms at the Civil Desk of the Circuit Court where you live (DCI Report, Petition/Motion, and Financial Statement). Don't forget to sign and date the forms.

A filing fee and sometimes a Master's fee are required at this time. If you are requesting the Waiver of Fees, you must file that Motion along with your forms now. (If you have already filed and been granted the Waiver of fees—then file the granted Waiver at this time in order to avoid paying the fees.)

If you plan to serve the other party out of state, ask the Clerk for a 60-day *Writ of Summons*. If you plan to serve the other party out of the country, ask the Clerk for a 90-day Writ of Summons.

STEP 4 —**Service.**

Follow instructions on Page 94.

You must serve the other party correctly after you file your Petition/Motion and receive your Writ of Summons, or your case cannot go forward.

STEP 5 —**Return Completed Affidavit of Service, Dom. Rel. 55 or 56.**

Have the person who served the defendant complete Dom. Rel. 55 and return it to you for filing with the Clerk. If service was by Certified Mail you complete and return Dom. Rel. 56.

If service was done by a Sheriff in Maryland, the Clerk will have sent the Summons and Petition directly to the Sheriff. And the Sheriff will return the Affidavit of Service and Writ of Summons directly to the Clerk for filing.

STEP 6 —**Request for Default if No Answer is Filed:**

If your (ex-)spouse is served in Maryland, s/he must answer within 30 days. If your (ex-)spouse is served in another state, s/he must answer within 60 days. If your (ex-)spouse is served in another country, s/he must answer within 90 days.

If your (ex-)spouse has not filed an Answer by the appropriate time, complete and file a *Request for Order of Default,* Dom. Rel. 54. (Follow step-by-step instructions on page 120.) You will receive a signed copy of the granted Order of Default in the mail.

STEP 7 —**Request for Master's Hearing or Trial on the Merits.**

After you have received either an Answer or an Order of Default, file a *Request for Master's Hearing*, Dom. Rel. 51, or a *Request for Trial on the Merits*, Dom. Rel. 52, so that a court date will be set. In some counties you will not have to file a *Request for a Master's Hearing*; you simply contact the Master directly and set up a date for the hearing. The Master's fee varies from county to county in Maryland.

STEP 8 —**Prepare for the Hearing.**

Whether or not the other party answered, send him/her a notice of the date, time and place of the hearing and either file a copy of the notice with the Court or bring a copy to the hearing.

Hearing Checklist. When you come to court you should have:
- ✓__Completed Child Support Guidelines Worksheet (if requesting a change of custody)
- ✓__A copy of any previous child support Order
- ✓__Your last 3 pay stubs
- ✓__Your last 2 tax returns
- ✓__Any witnesses who you think may help the court to see why this change is best for your child(ren)

COMPLAINT FOR ABSOLUTE DIVORCE
(Dom. Rel. 20)

If you want the court to grant you a complete dissolution (ending) of a marriage, you are asking the court to grant you an *absolute divorce*. After the court issues a *Judgment of Absolute Divorce*, you can remarry.

If you cannot afford court fees, you may be eligible for the Waiver of Fees (see instructions on page 93).

Complete 11 steps to secure an uncontested absolute divorce.

STEP 1 —Complete Dom. Rel. 20: Complaint for Absolute Divorce, *Page 1*–Fill in both your name, as Plaintiff, and your spouse's name, as Defendant. Then, fill in *current* addresses and telephone numbers for both. *Do not* fill in where it says "Case No."

Line 1: After filling in your name in the space provided, fill in the month, day, and year of your marriage. In the second blank, fill in the city or county and the state where you were married. Circle whether you were married in a religious or a civil ceremony.

Line 2: Check off all statements that apply in your case and fill in the blanks.

Line 3: If you check off, "We have no children together...," remember to skip lines 4 and 5. If you check off, "My spouse and I are the parents...," write in the full names of all the children you and your spouse had together and their dates of birth.

Line 4: Fill in the name of the person with whom those children listed above now live.

Line 5: Check the box for the type of custody or visitation you want and fill in the names of the children involved.

Line 6: Circle whether or not you are seeking alimony and state why.

Line 7: If you are asking the court to make a decision as to your property, check off the kinds of property you and your spouse have. If you or your spouse have debts, you may check the box marked "Debts" and attach a list of the debts to this form.

Page 2—**Line 8:** Check all the grounds for divorce that apply and fill in the blanks. Choosing a certain ground will not necessarily result in a divorce being granted.

Two-year Separation—If you and your spouse have lived apart from each other for two years without sexual intercourse and there is no reasonable hope of getting back together, you may check this ground. There are some important things to remember: during the last two years, if you and your spouse lived together at all, or if you have had sexual intercourse with your spouse during that time, or if you spent even one night under the same roof, you cannot get an absolute divorce based on a two-year separation. (For example, if you have been separated from your spouse for two years, but one night a year ago you had sexual intercourse with your spouse, then you have only been separated for one year.)

Voluntary Separation—One year (12 months) ago you and your spouse agreed to separate with the idea of ending your marriage. For that entire year you and your spouse lived in separate homes and did not have sexual intercourse with each other. There can be no reasonable hope of getting back together. You may check this ground if *all* of these statements are true.

Adultery—If your spouse has had voluntary sexual intercourse with a person other than you, you may check this ground for an absolute divorce. You must be able to prove that your spouse committed the act of adultery or that he or she had disposition and opportunity. Disposition is when your spouse and someone of the opposite sex acted romantically towards each other. Opportunity is a specific chance to have sexual intercourse with that person.

Actual Desertion—If your spouse left you more than 12 months ago with the intention of ending the marriage *and* you and your spouse have not had sexual intercourse with each other during that time, then you may check this ground.

Constructive Desertion—If one year ago your spouse forced you to leave the home by making it impossible for the two of you to live together in safety, with health and self-respect *and* you and your spouse have not had sexual intercourse with each other during this time, then you may check this ground.

Criminal Conviction of a Felony or Misdemeanor—This ground is explained on the form.

Insanity—This ground is explained on the form.

At the bottom of the form, check off everything you want. *If you fail to ask for alimony and/or property before the divorce, you will not be able to* **ever** *get it.* The court will not necessarily give you what you asked for.

If you have a Separation Agreement or Marital Property Agreement, add a checkbox in pen, check and write the following words in pen: "The attached Separation Agreement shall be incorporated but not merged into the final Judicial Divorce Decree."

Don't forget to check the box that requests that your former name be restored. If you do not change your name as part of the divorce proceeding, you will have to go to the expense of filing a separate change of name action after your divorce.

STEP 2 —Complete Other Court Documents.

> Property Settlement Agreement (if you have one)
> Financial Statement (Alimony or Child Support), Dom. Rel. 30 or 31.

You may need to complete and attach to the Complaint one or both of the above.

STEP 3 —Make Copies.

> Make 3 copies of the Complaint, Property Settlement, and Financial Statement.

STEP 4 —File your Forms and Pay the Filing Fee.

> File the original copies of the above forms at the Civil Desk of the Circuit Court where you live (Complaint, Property Settlement, and Financial Statement). Don't forget to sign and date the forms.
>
> A filing fee and sometimes a Master's fee are required at this time. If you are requesting the Waiver of Fees, you must file that Motion along with your forms now. (If you have already filed and been granted the Waiver of fees—then file the granted Waiver at this time in order to avoid paying the fees.)
>
> If you plan to serve the other party out of state, ask the Clerk for a 60-day *Writ of Summons*. If you plan to serve the other party out of the United States, ask the Clerk for a 90-day Writ of Summons.

STEP 5 —Service.

> Follow instructions on Page 94.
>
> *You must serve the other party correctly after you file your Complaint and receive your Writ of Summons, or your case cannot go forward.*

STEP 6 —Return Completed Affidavit of Service, Dom. Rel. 55 or 56.

> Have the person who served the defendant complete Dom. Rel. 55 and return it to you for filing with the Clerk. If service was by Certified Mail you complete and return Dom. Rel. 56.
>
> If service was done by a Sheriff in Maryland, the Clerk will have sent the Summons and Complaint directly to the Sheriff. And the Sheriff will return the Affidavit of Service and Writ of Summons directly to the Clerk for filing.

STEP 7 —Request for Default if No Answer is Filed.

> If your spouse is served in Maryland, s/he must answer within 30 days.
> If your spouse is served in another state, s/he must answer within 60 days.
> If your spouse is served in another country, s/he must answer within 90 days.
>
> If your spouse has not filed an Answer by the appropriate time, complete and file a *Request for Order of Default*, Dom. Rel. 54. (Follow step-by-step instructions on page 120.) You will receive a signed copy of the granted Order of Default in the mail.

STEP 8 —Request for Master's Hearing or Trial on the Merits.

> After you have received an Answer or an Order of Default, file a *Request for Master's Hearing*, Dom. Rel. 51, or a *Request for Trial on the Merits*, Dom.

Rel. 52, so that a court date will be set. In some counties you will not have to file a *Request for a Master's Hearing*; you simply contact the Master directly and set up a date for the hearing. The Master's fee will vary depending on the county within Maryland. A typical fee is $75.00 for an uncontested Master's Hearing.

STEP 9 —**Marital and Non-marital Property.**

If property is an issue you may have to complete a *Joint Statement of Parties Concerning Marital and Non-marital Property*, Dom. Rel. 33, before your court date.

STEP 10 —**Prepare for the Hearing.**

Whether or not your spouse answered, send him/her a notice of the date, time, and place of the hearing and either file a copy of the notice with the Court or bring a copy to the hearing. Request subpoenas from the Clerk for any witnesses or documents needed at the hearing.

> *Hearing Checklist.* When you come to court you should have:
> ✓__Marriage license (original or certified copy)
> ✓__Completed Child Support Guidelines
> ✓__A copy of any previous child support Order
> ✓__Your last three pay stubs
> ✓__Your last two tax returns
> ✓__Joint Statement of Parties Concerning Marital and Non-Marital Property
> ✓__Copy of any Separation or Marital Settlement Agreement
> ✓__The "Blue Form" (see STEP 11 below)
> ✓__Your corroborative witness

At the hearing for Absolute Divorce, you will need a *corroborative witness*. This is a person who testifies for you and backs up your story. The witness gives his/her testimony based on the facts s/he saw or heard. The one important exception is that your witness can testify to what your spouse (but not you) told him/her. *Carefully read the instructions on* The Hearing *in Part 1 of this book.*

UNCONTESTED MATTER: Examples of the most commonly used uncontested grounds are:

Two-Year Separation: Your witness should be someone who knows you well and has frequent contact with you. Your witness must testify under oath that s/he knows:
> ➤you and your spouse are married to each other;
> ➤you and your spouse have been separated for two years;
> ➤there is no reasonable hope of your getting back together;
> ➤if there is an Order of default; and
> ➤whether or not your spouse is in the military.

If possible, you should not pick someone to be your witness whom your spouse dislikes. (For example, you should avoid using a new "special" friend as your corroborative witness.)

Voluntary Separation: Your witness should be someone who knows you well and has frequent contact with you. Your witness must testify under oath that s/he knows:

➤you and your spouse;

➤you are married to each other;

➤you and your spouse *BOTH* voluntarily agreed to separate;

➤you and your spouse have been separated for one year;

➤there is no reasonable hope of your getting back together;

➤if there is an Order of default; and

➤whether or not your spouse is in the military.

If you and your spouse signed a separation agreement under oath (sworn), which says that you separated "mutually and voluntarily" as of a certain date (at least a year ago), then your witness does not have to know it was voluntary.

Even if you have this type of separation agreement, you will still need a witness to testify to the other requirements.

CONTESTED MATTER: If you have any contested matters, you should seek an attorney well before the court date.

STEP 11 —Judgment of Divorce.

After your hearing, the court will prepare a *Judgment of Divorce.* (In some counties you may have to prepare the Judgment of Divorce document. If so, ask the Clerk of Court for a sample form.)

Lastly, you will have to complete a "Blue Form"* which you file with the court. You secure the Blue Form from the Clerk's Office. This is an "official form" that amends your records with the State of Maryland and notifies the State that you are now divorced and no longer married. See sample form in "Forms" section following the instructions.

COMPLAINT FOR LIMITED DIVORCE
(Dom. Rel. 21)

If you do not want the court to grant you a complete dissolution (ending) of a marriage, but you have issues you want the court to settle, then you can ask for a *limited divorce*. After the court issues the *Judgment of Limited Divorce,* you *cannot remarry* unless you later get an *absolute divorce.*

If you cannot afford court fees, you may be eligible for the Waiver of Fees (see instructions on page 93).

Complete 11 steps to secure an uncontested limited divorce:

STEP 1 —Complete Complaint for Limited Divorce, Dom. Rel. 21.
Page 1–Fill in both your name, as Plaintiff, and your spouse's name, as Defendant. Then, fill in *current* addresses and telephone numbers for both. *Do not* fill in where it says "Case No."

Line 1: After filling in your name in the space provided, fill in the month, day, and year of your marriage. In the second blank, fill in the city or county and the state where you were married. Circle whether you were married in a religious or a civil ceremony.

Line 2: Check off all statements that apply in your case and fill in the blanks.

Line 3: If you check off, "We have no children together...," remember to skip lines 4 and 5. If you check off, "My spouse and I are the parents...," write in the full names of all the children you and your spouse had together and their dates of birth.

Line 4: Fill in the name of the person with whom those children listed above now live.

Line 5: Check the box for the type of custody or visitation you want and fill in the names of the children involved.

Line 6: Circle whether or not you are seeking alimony and state why.

Line 7: If you are asking the court to make a decision as to your property, check off the kinds of property you and your spouse have. If you or your spouse have debts, you may check the box marked "Debts" and attach a list of the debts to this form.

Page 2–**Line 8:** Check all the grounds for limited divorce that apply and fill in the blanks. Choosing a certain ground will not necessarily result in a limited divorce being granted.

Cruelty/Excessively Vicious Conduct Against Me—If your spouse has endangered your safety or health more than once, you may check this ground. However, one incident may be enough if it was very violent and your spouse intended to harm you. The court will want you to prove that you cannot live with your spouse safely.

Cruelty/Excessively Vicious Conduct Against My Children—This ground is the same as the above ground except that your spouse is being cruel to your child(ren) instead of you.

Actual Desertion—If your spouse has left you with the intention of ending the marriage *and* you and your spouse have not had sexual intercourse with each other since that time, you may check this ground.

Constructive Desertion—If your spouse has forced you to leave the home by making it impossible for the two of you to live together in safety, with health and self-respect *and* you and your spouse have not had sexual intercourse with each other since you left, then you may check this ground.

Voluntary Separation—You and your spouse have agreed to separate with the idea of ending your marriage. You and your spouse live in separate homes and have not had sexual intercourse with each other. There is no reasonable hope of your getting back together. If *all* of these statements are true, then you may check this ground.

At the bottom, check off everything you want. *If you fail to ask for alimony and/or property before the divorce, you will not be able to **ever** get it.* The court will not necessarily give you what you asked for.

If you have a Separation Agreement or Marital Property Agreement, add a checkbox in pen, check and write the following words in pen: "The attached Separation Agreement shall be incorporated but not merged into the final Judicial Divorce Decree."

STEP 2 —Complete Other Court Documents.
    Property Settlement Agreement, if you have one, and
    Financial Statement (Alimony or Child Support), Dom. Rel. 30 or 31
You may need to complete and attach to the Complaint one or both of the above.

STEP 3 —Make Copies.
    Make 3 copies of the Complaint, Property Settlement, and Financial Statement.

STEP 4 —File your Forms and Pay the Filing Fee.
    File the original copies of the above forms at the Civil Desk of the Circuit Court where you live (Complaint, Property Settlement, and Financial Statement). Don't forget to sign and date the forms.
    A filing fee and sometimes a Master's fee are required at this time. If you are requesting the Waiver of Fees, you must file that Motion along with your forms now. (If you have already filed and been granted the Waiver of fees—then file the granted Waiver at this time in order to avoid paying the fees.)

If you plan to serve the other party out of state, ask the Clerk for a 60-day *Writ of Summons*. If you plan to serve the other party out of the United States, ask the Clerk for a 90-day Writ of Summons.

STEP 5 —Service.

Follow instructions on Page 94.

You must serve the other party correctly after you file your Complaint and receive your Writ of Summons, or your case cannot go forward.

STEP 6 —Return Completed Affidavit of Service, Dom. Rel. 55 or 56.

Have the person who served the defendant complete Dom. Rel. 55 and return it to you for filing with the Clerk. If service was by Certified Mail you complete and return Dom. Rel. 56.

If service was done by a Sheriff in Maryland, the Clerk will have sent the Summons and Complaint directly to the Sheriff. And the Sheriff will return the Affidavit of Service and Writ of Summons directly to the Clerk for filing.

STEP 7 —Request for Default if No Answer is Filed.

If your spouse is served in Maryland, s/he must answer within 30 days.

If your spouse is served in another state, s/he must answer within 60 days.

If your spouse is served in another country, s/he must answer within 90 days.

If your (ex-)spouse has not filed an Answer by the appropriate time, complete and file a *Request for Order of Default,* Dom. Rel. 54. (Follow step-by-step instructions on page 120.) You will receive a signed copy of the granted Order of Default in the mail.

STEP 8 —Request for Master's Hearing or Trial on the Merits.

After you have received an Answer or an Order of Default, file a *Request for Master's Hearing*, Dom. Rel. 51, or a *Request for Trial on the Merits*, Dom. Rel. 52, so that a court date will be set. In some counties you will not have to file a *Request for a Master's Hearing*; you simply contact the Master directly and set up a date for the hearing. The Master's fee varies from county to county in Maryland. A typical fee is $75.00 for an uncontested Master's Hearing.

STEP 9 —Marital and Non-marital Property.

If property is an issue you may have to complete a *Joint Statement of Parties Concerning Marital and Non-marital Property*, Dom. Rel. 33, before your court date.

STEP 10 —Prepare for the Hearing.

Whether or not your spouse answered, send him/her a notice of the date, time and place of the hearing and file a copy of the notice with the Court or bring a copy to the hearing. Request subpoenas from the Clerk for any witnesses or documents needed at the hearing.

Hearing Checklist. When you come to court you should have:

✓__Marriage license (original or certified copy)
✓__Completed Child Support Guidelines Worksheet
✓__A copy of any previous child support Order
✓__Your last three pay stubs
✓__Your last two tax returns
✓__Joint Statement of Parties Concerning Marital and Non-marital Property
✓__Copy of any Separation or Marital Settlement Agreement
✓__The "Blue Form" (see STEP 11 below)
✓__Your corroborative witness

At the hearing for Limited Divorce, you will need a *corroborative witness.* This is a person who testifies for you and backs up your story. The witness gives his/her testimony based on the facts he/she saw or heard. The one important exception is that your witness can testify to what your spouse (but not you) told him/her.*Carefully read the instructions on* The Hearing *in Part 1 of this book.*

UNCONTESTED MATTER: The most commonly used uncontested ground is:

Voluntary Separation: Your witness should be someone who knows you well and has frequent contact with you. Your witness must testify under oath that s/he knows:

➤you and your spouse;
➤you are married to each other;
➤you and your spouse BOTH voluntarily agreed to separate;
➤you and your spouse have been separated for one year;
➤there is no reasonable hope of your getting back together;
➤if there is an Order of default, and
➤whether or not your spouse is in the military.

If you and your spouse signed a separation agreement under oath (sworn), which says that you separated "mutually and voluntarily" as of a certain date (at least a year ago), then your witness does not have to know it was voluntary.

Even if you have this type of separation agreement, you will still need a witness to testify to the other requirements.

CONTESTED MATTER: If you have any contested matters, you should seek an attorney well before the court date.

STEP 11 —Judgment of Divorce.

After your hearing, the court will prepare a *Judgment of Divorce.* (In some counties you may have to prepare the Judgment of Divorce document. If so, ask the Clerk of Court for a sample form.)

ANSWER TO COMPLAINT, MOTION, PETITION
(Dom. Rel. 50)

If you have been served with divorce, custody, visitation, or child support papers, you may need to file an *Answer*. You should file an Answer if you disagree with anything in the papers filed by the other side, and you want the court to hear your side of the story. If you do not file an Answer, the court may give the other side what s/he has asked for without hearing what you have to say. If the case is uncontested, you still may want to file an Answer because that will speed up the process.

If you are filing an Answer, you must file in the county where the Complaint, Petition or Motion was filed. If you think the other side filed in the wrong county, you can ask the court, in writing, to move the case to a different county. This is a situation that may require a lawyer's assistance.

Complete 8 steps to file an Answer.

STEP 1 —Complete the Form:
Dom. Rel. 50: Answer to Complaint, Motion, Petition.

Page 1–Fill in:
the name of the court and the case number as it appears on the Writ of Summons you received

the plaintiff's and defendant's names exactly as they appear on the paper you are answering

the current addresses and telephone numbers for both (if your address is different from the one listed on the papers filed by the other side, be sure to tell that to the Clerk of the Court when you file your papers)

your name after the word "I" followed by the name of the Complaint, Petition, or Motion that you are answering.

Lines 1 through 5: You must answer each numbered paragraph of the papers filed by the other side. Check off all statements that apply in your case.

Page 2—**Lines 6 through 8:** Continue to answer each numbered paragraph of the papers filed by the other side. Check off all statements that apply in your case.

Line 9: If you have other facts that you want the Court to consider, write them here. If there is not enough space, you may attach a separate piece of paper, but be sure to follow the instructions below.

In the Section beginning "FOR THESE REASONS:" Check each box that applies to you.

STEP 2 —Other Court Documents.

Dom. Rel. 30 or 31, Financial Statement (Alimony or Child Support) if you or the other party are asking for alimony or child support.

Civil–Domestic Case Information (DCI) Report (if needed).

You may need to complete and attach to the Answer one or both of the above.

STEP 3 —Make Copies.

Make 3 copies of the Answer, DCI Report, and Financial Statement.

STEP 4 —File Your Forms.

File the original copies of the above forms at the Civil Desk of the Circuit Court where you live (DCI Report, Answer, and Financial Statement). Don't forget to sign and date the forms.

STEP 5 —Service.

You must mail a copy of the Answer and everything you are filing to the other side. If the other side has an attorney, mail the papers to that attorney. Fill in the section, "CERTIFICATE OF SERVICE," located at the bottom of Page 2 of the Answer form.

STEP 6 —Marital and Non-marital Property.

If you are involved in a divorce case, you may have to complete a Joint Statement of Parties Concerning Marital and Non-marital Property (Dom. Rel. 33), before your hearing date.

STEP 7 —Child Support.

You may have to fill out a *Child Support Guidelines Worksheet* for the hearing. Ask the Clerk of the Court how to get one. You can check your calculations on the Child Support Guidelines Worksheet by using the Child Support Calculator that is maintained on the Internet by the People's Law Library of Maryland at http://www.peoples-law.com.

STEP 8 —Counterclaim

If you want something different from what the other side wants, you should file a Counterclaim. Follow these steps:

Complete the Counterclaim on Page 3 of Dom. Rel. 50 and any other required Dom. Rel. forms.

Make 3 copies of the Counterclaim and its related Dom. Rel. forms.

File the original copies of the Counterclaim and the forms with the Clerk of Court. Don't forget to sign your name and date the forms.

You must mail a copy of the Counterclaim and everything you are filing to the other side. If the other side has an attorney, mail the papers to that attorney.

Fill in the section, "CERTIFICATE OF SERVICE," for the Counterclaim at the bottom of Page 3.

REQUEST FOR ORDER OF DEFAULT
Dom. Rel. 54

After service has been made, you must give the other side an opportunity to answer. You must wait 30 days for an Answer if the other side is served in Maryland, 60 days if the other side is served out side of the State, and 90 days if the other side is served outside of the United States. If the other side has not filed an Answer within the required time, you must file a *Request for Order of Default* (Dom. Rel. 54) so that your case can go forward.

Complete 4 steps to file a Request for Order of Default.

STEP 1 —Complete the Form
Dom. Rel. 54: Request for Order of Default

Page 1—Fill in the case number *exactly* as it appears on your other papers; your name and the other side's name in the spaces provided; and the *current* addresses and telephone numbers for both.

After *"Request for Order of Default:"* Fill in your name, the other side's name, and the current or last known address of the other side. Date and sign the form on the lines provided.

After *"Non-Military Affidavit:"* Make sure each of the statements in lines 1 through 4 is true. If even one of the statements is not true, you will not be able to use this form and you should see an attorney. If all the statements are true, fill in the other side's name. Date and sign the form on the lines provided.

Page 2—Fill in your name, the other side's name, and the correct case number in the spaces provided. *Do not fill out* any other part of Page 2.

STEP 2 —Make copies.
Make 2 copies of the Request.

STEP 3 —File Your Form.
File the original copies of the above forms at the Civil Desk of the Circuit Court where you live. You do not have to mail a copy of this paper to the other side. Don't forget to sign and date the forms.

STEP 4 —If Order of Default Is Signed by the Court
If the court grants your Request, a judge will sign the Order of Default and a copy will be returned to you.

The other side has 30 days to ask the court to set aside the Order and allow a late response. After that time has passed, the other side generally will not be allowed to contest the case, and you may now proceed with your action.

The Forms

Do not make any changes to the forms. Make copies of all of the forms as they appear in this book—*on one-side of the sheet only* (except for Dom. Rel. 53, Show Cause Order, which should be copied with the "Form" on the front side and the "Notice" on the back of the same sheet.) The forms appear in the following order beginning on the next page:

◊ "Blue Form." Maryland State Department of Health and Mental Hygiene: Report of Absolute Divorce or Annulment of Marriage (*Obtain from the Clerk.*)

◊ Dom. Rel. 1, Complaint for Child Support
◊ Dom. Rel. 2, Petition for Contempt (Failure to Pay Child Support)
◊ Dom. Rel. 3, Petition for Contempt (Denial of Visitation)
◊ Dom. Rel. 4, Complaint for Custody
◊ Dom. Rel. 5, Complaint for Visitation
◊ Dom. Rel. 6, Petition/Motion to Modify Child Support
◊ Dom. Rel. 7, Petition/Motion to Modify Custody/Visitation
◊ Dom. Rel. 20, Complaint for Absolute Divorce
◊ Dom. Rel. 21, Complaint for Limited Divorce
◊ Dom. Rel. 30, Financial Statement (Child Support)
◊ Dom. Rel. 31, Financial Statement (Alimony or Child Support)
◊ Dom. Rel. 32, Motion for Waiver of Prepayment of Filing Fees and Other Court Costs
◊ Dom. Rel. 33, Joint Statement of Parties Concerning Marital and Non-Marital Property
◊ Dom. Rel. 50, Answer to Complaint/Petition/Motion (with Counterclaim)
◊ Dom. Rel. 51, Request for Master's Hearing
◊ Dom. Rel. 52, Request for Trial on the Merits
◊ Dom. Rel. 53, Show Cause Order (Form to be Completed by Court)
◊ Dom. Rel. 54, Request for Order of Default
◊ Dom. Rel. 55, Affidavit of Service (Private Process)
◊ Dom. Rel. 56, Affidavit of Service (Certified Mail)
◊ Dom. Rel. 57, Order
◊ Earnings Withholding Order (with Instruction for Earnings Withholding)

Other Forms (Not Shown in Book)—obtain from the Clerk, when needed.
⇨ Child Support Guidelines Worksheet
⇨ Civil–Domestic Case Information (DCI) Report
⇨ Differentiated Case Management Form.

MARGIN RESERVED FOR BINDING

AUTHORITY FOR THIS REPORT IS FOUND IN ARTICLE 62, SECTION 18 (a) (b)

Entries should be typewritten or printed in permanent-type ink.
(Do not report limited divorces.)

MARYLAND STATE DEPARTMENT OF HEALTH AND MENTAL HYGIENE

Division of Vital Records
4201 Patterson Avenue
Baltimore, MD 21215-2299

REPORT OF ABSOLUTE DIVORCE OR ANNULMENT OF MARRIAGE

	HUSBAND	WIFE		
1. NAME	(First) (Middle) (Last)		2. AGE	3. Place of Birth (State or foreign country)
4. RESIDENCE	(City) (County) (State)		5. Number of this Marriage (First, Second, Third)	6. Race White ☐ Negro ☐ Other ☐ (Specify)
7. MAIDEN NAME	(First) (Middle) (Last)		8. AGE	9. Place of Birth (State or foreign country)
10. RESIDENCE	(City) (County) (State)		11. Number of this Marriage (First, Second Third)	12. Race White ☐ Negro ☐ Other ☐ (Specify)

MARRIAGE PARTICULARS

13. Place of this marriage	(County) (State or foreign country)		14. Date of this Marriage (Month) (Day) (Year)
15. Plaintiff Husband ☐ Wife ☐	16. Decree granted to 1. Husband ☐ 2. Wife ☐	17. Legal grounds for decree	18. Total number of living children .... No. under 18 years of age

CLERK OF CIRCUIT COURT

19. Name of Attorney for Plaintiff	(Street Address) (City or Town) (County) (State)
Docket No.	Folio No.
I hereby certify that the above persons were divorced and decree signed on: (Month) (Day) (Year)	Type of Decree 1. Absolute (A Vinculo) ☐ 2. Annulment ☐
Name of Clerk of Court	Signature of Clerk of Court	County of Decree

INSTRUCTIONS: TO THE CLERK OF THE CIRCUIT COURT: When a petition for absolute divorce or annulment is filed, please hand a copy of this form to the attorney for completion of items No. 1 through No. 19. When the decree is signed check completeness of these items, execute the bottom section and mail to Maryland State Department of Health & Mental Hygiene of Vital Records, 4201 Patterson Avenue, Baltimore, Maryland 21215-2299 on or before the 10th of the month next succeeding the divorce.

TO THE ATTORNEY: Please complete items No. 1 through No. 19 of the Report of Absolute Divorce or Annulment of Marriage and ask your client to verify the information. RETURN THE FORM TO THE CLERK OF THE COURT FOR CERTIFICATION.

Circuit Court for _____ Case No._____

_____
City or County

_____   _____
Name   Name

_____ VS. _____

Street Address   Apt #   Street Address   Apt #

_____   _____

City   State   Zip Code   City   State   Zip Code

_____   _____

Area Code   Telephone   Area Code   Telephone

Plaintiff   Defendant

COMPLAINT FOR CHILD SUPPORT
(Dom. Rel. 1)

I, _____ , representing myself, state that:

1.   I am the mother/father or _____ of
       _{Circle One}

       the following minor child(ren) or adult disabled child(ren):

_____ _____   _____ _____
Name   Date of Birth   Name   Date of Birth

_____ _____   _____ _____
Name   Date of Birth   Name   Date of Birth

_____ _____   _____ _____
Name   Date of Birth   Name   Date of Birth

2.   The child(ren) live(s) at _____
       with _____

3.   The _____ is the mother/father of the child(ren) and (check all that apply):

       ( )   is not making child support payments.
       ( )   is not making regular child support payments.
       ( )   is not making child support payments in an amount required by the Maryland
       Child Support Guidelines.

FOR THESE REASONS, I request the Court (check all that apply):

       ( )   Order _____ to pay child support payments in an amount
       required by the Maryland Child Support Guidelines.

       ( )   Order child support to be paid by earnings withholding order (check one):
               ( )   Through the local support enforcement agency.

( )   Directly to me.

( )   Order _____ to provide health insurance for the child(ren).

(X)   Order any other appropriate relief.

I solemnly affirm under the penalties of perjury, that the contents of the foregoing paper are true to the best of my knowledge, information and belief.

_____
Date

_____
Name

**IMPORTANT: YOU MUST COMPLETE A FINANCIAL STATEMENT WITH THIS FORM
(USE FORM DOM REL 30 OR DOM REL 31)
IF YOU ARE REQUESTING A WITHHOLDING ORDER, YOU MUST ATTACHED IT
TO THIS COMPLAINT**

Circuit Court for _____ Case No._____

City or County

Name _____ Name _____

Street Address _____ Apt # _____ VS. Street Address _____ Apt # _____

City _____ State _____ Zip Code _____ City _____ State _____ Zip Code _____

Area Code _____ Telephone _____ Area Code _____ Telephone _____

Plaintiff   Defendant

PETITION FOR CONTEMPT
(Failure to Pay Child Support)
(Dom.Rel. 2)

I,_____ , representing myself, state that:

1. I am the mother/father or _____ of
    My Name   Circle One
    the following minor child(ren) or adult disabled child(ren):

    _____ _____   _____ _____
    Name   Date of Birth   Name   Date of Birth

    _____ _____   _____ _____
    Name   Date of Birth   Name   Date of Birth

    _____ _____   _____ _____
    Name   Date of Birth   Name   Date of Birth

2. On _____ the Circuit Court for _____ issued an Order in   case number
    _____ ordering _____ to pay $_____ weekly/biweekly/monthly

    toward the support of the child(ren).

3. _____ has not made child support payments as required by the Order.

4. $_____ child support is due as of _____

5. I do/do not want the court to order jail time to enforce its Order. [circle one].

FOR THESE REASONS, I request the Court issue a Show cause Order, issue an Order of Contempt for failure to pay child support, order payment of current child support and arrearages, and order any other appropriate relief.

_____   _____
Date   Name

IMPORTANT: YOU MUST ATTACH A SHOW CAUSE ORDER TO THIS FORM
(USE FORM DOM REL 53)

Circuit Court for _____   Case No._____

City or County

_____   _____
Name   Name

_____   VS.   _____
Street Address   Apt #   Street Address   Apt #

_____   _____
City   State   Zip Code   City   State   Zip Code

_____   _____
Area Code   Telephone   Area Code   Telephone

               Plaintiff   Defendant

PETITION FOR CONTEMPT
(DENIAL OF VISITATION)
(Dom.Rel.3)

I, _____ , representing myself, state that:

1.   On _____ the Circuit Court for _____ issued an Order in case

      number _____ granting me visitation.

2.   Since then, I have been denied visitation with the children as ordered. The

      details of the denials are: _____

      _____

      _____

3.   I last visited with the child(ren) on _____

4.   _____ is now in contempt for failing to obey the Order.

5.   I do/do not want the Court to order jail time to enforce its order. [circle one].

FOR THESE REASONS, I request the Court issue a Show cause Order, find _____ in

Contempt, enforce visitation, and order any other appropriate relief relating to visitation with the

child(ren), including: _____

_____

_____

_____   _____
    Date   Name

IMPORTANT: YOU MUST ATTACH A SHOW CAUSE ORDER TO THIS FORM(USE FORM DOM REL 53)

Circuit Court for _____ Case No. _____
City or County

Name _____		Name _____
Street Address _____ Apt. #	VS.	Street Address _____ Apt. #
( )		( )
City State Zip Code Area Telephone		City State Zip Code Area Telephone
Code		Code
Plaintiff		*Defendant No. 1*

Name _____

Street Address _____ Apt. #
( )
City   State   Zip Code   Area   Telephone
Code
Defendant No. 2

COMPLAINT FOR CUSTODY
(Dom.Rel. 4)

I, _____ , representing myself, state that:
My name

1.   I am the mother/father or _____
     Circle One   Relationship (for example, aunt, grandfather, guardian, etc.)

     of the following minor child(ren):

Name	Date of Birth	Name	Date of Birth
_____	_____	_____	_____
Name	Date of Birth	Name	Date of Birth
_____	_____	_____	_____
Name	Date of Birth	Name	Date of Birth

2.   _____ is the mother/father or _____
     Defendant   Circle One   Relationship

     of the child(ren). Defendant No. 2 is the mother/father of the child(ren).
                                            Circle One

3.   The child(ren) live(s) at_____
                                            Address

     with_____ .
         Name of Person

4.   I know of the following cases concerning the child(ren) (such as paternity, divorce of the

     child(ren)'s parents, custody, visitation, or juvenile court cases):

Court	Kind of Case	Year Filed	Results or Status (if you know)
_____	_____	_____	_____
_____	_____	_____	_____
_____	_____	_____	_____
_____	_____	_____	_____

5. It is in the best interests of the child(ren) to be in my custody because: _____

_____

_____

_____

_____

_____

_____

_____

FOR THESE REASONS, I request the Court (check all that apply):

☑ Grant me custody of the child(ren) and

    ☐ Allow _____ to visit with the child(ren).
                   Name(s)

    ☐ Allow _____ to visit with the child(ren) on
                   Name(s)

    the following terms:_____

_____

_____

    ☐ Allow no visitation because _____
                                     Reasons

☐ Order _____ to pay health insurance for child(ren).
           Name(s)

☐ Order _____ to pay child support (attach Financial
           Name(s)

Statement. Use Form Dom.Rel. 30 or Dom.Rel. 31).

☐ (State other requests relating to the children) _____

_____

_____

☑ Order any other appropriate relief.

_____   _____
      Date   Name

Circuit Court for _____ Case No. _____
                        City or County

Name				VS.	Name			
Street Address			Apt. #		Street Address			Apt. #
			( )					( )
City	State	Zip Code	Area Code Telephone		City	State	Zip Code	Area Code Telephone
		Plaintiff					**Defendant**	

COMPLAINT FOR VISITATION
(Dom.Rel. 5)

I, _____ , representing myself, state that:
        My name

1. I am the mother/father or _____
                  Circle One   Relationship (for example, aunt, grandfather, guardian, etc.)

    of the following minor child(ren):

Name	Date of Birth	Name	Date of Birth
Name	Date of Birth	Name	Date of Birth
Name	Date of Birth	Name	Date of Birth

2. The child(ren) live at _____
                                                        Address

    with_____ .
              Name and Relationship to Child(ren)

3. I know of the following cases concerning the child(ren) (such as paternity, divorce of the

    child(ren)'s parents, custody, visitation, or juvenile court cases:

Court	Kind of Case	Year Filed	Results or Status (if you know)
_____	_____	_____	_____
_____	_____	_____	_____
_____	_____	_____	_____

4. It is in the best interests of the child(ren) to visit with me because: _____

    _____

    _____

    _____

FOR THESE REASONS, I request the Court grant me reasonable visitation as follows: _____

_____

_____

_____ and any other appropriate relief.

_____   _____
            Date   Name

Dom.Rel. 5 (2 96)

Circuit Court for _____ Case No. _____
                        City or County

Name _____	Name _____
Street Address _____ Apt. # ___	Street Address _____ Apt. # ___
	VS.	

City ____ State ___ Zip Code ___ Area Code ( ) ___ Telephone ___   City ____ State ___ Zip Code ___ Area Code ( ) ___ Telephone ___

Plaintiff   **Defendant**

PETITION/MOTION TO MODIFY CHILD SUPPORT
(Dom.Rel. 6)

I, _____ , representing myself, state that:
                     My name

1. I am the mother/father or _____ of:
              Circle One   Relationship (for example, aunt, grandfather, guardian, etc.)

    _____ _____   _____ _____
         Name   Date of Birth   Name   Date of Birth

    _____ _____   _____ _____
         Name   Date of Birth   Name   Date of Birth

    _____ _____   _____ _____
         Name   Date of Birth   Name   Date of Birth

2. On _____ the Circuit Court for _____ issued an
              Date   City or County

    Order in case number _____ , ordering _____
                                                              Name

    to pay $ _____ weekly/biweekly/monthly toward the support of the child(ren).
              Amount   Circle One

3. Since that Order, circumstances have changed (check all that apply):

    ☐   Expenses for the child(ren) have substantially increased.

    ☐   Expenses for the child(ren) have substantially decreased.

    ☐   Father/mother's income has substantially increased.
              Circle One

    ☐   Father/mother's income has substantially decreased.
              Circle One

    ☐   Child(ren) have reached the age of 18 years.

    ☐   Other changes have occurred (explain): _____

    _____

    _____

    _____

    _____

    _____

FOR THESE REASONS, I request the Court (check all that apply):

- ☐ Order an increase in child support.
- ☐ Order a decrease in child support.
- ☑ Order child support to be paid (check one):
  - ☐ Through the local support enforcement agency.
  - ☐ Directly to the person who has custody.
- ☐ Order _____ to provide health insurance for the child(ren).
      <small>Name</small>
- ☑ Order any other appropriate relief.

I solemnly affirm under the penalties of perjury that the contents of the foregoing paper are true to the best of my knowledge, information, and belief.

_____   _____
          Date   Name

IMPORTANT: YOU MUST COMPLETE A FINANCIAL STATEMENT WITH THIS FORM
(Use Form Dom.Rel. 30 or Dom.Rel. 31)

Circuit Court for _____ Case No. _____
                        City or County

Name _____   Name _____

Street Address _____ Apt. #   VS. Street Address _____ Apt. #
                                    ( )   ( )
City _____ State ___ Zip Code ___ Area ___ Telephone   City _____ State ___ Zip Code ___ Area ___ Telephone
                                   Code   Code
              Plaintiff   *Defendant No. 1*

                                                 Name _____

                                                 Street Address _____ Apt. #
                                                                                  ( )
                                                 City _____ State ___ Zip Code ___ Area ___ Telephone
                                                                                    Code
                                                              Defendant No. 2

PETITION/MOTION TO MODIFY ☐ CUSTODY ☐ VISITATION
            (Dom.Rel. 7)

I, _____ , representing myself, state that:
           My name

1.   I am the mother/father or _____ of :
                Circle One   Relationship (for example, aunt, grandfather, guardian, etc.)

     _____ _____   _____ _____
          Name   Date of Birth   Name   Date of Birth

     _____ _____   _____ _____
          Name   Date of Birth   Name   Date of Birth

     _____ _____   _____ _____
          Name   Date of Birth   Name   Date of Birth

2.   On _____ the Circuit Court for _____ issued
              Date   City or County

     an Order in case number _____ , granting custody of the child(ren) to_____

     _____ and visitation to_____ .

3.   Since the Order, circumstances have changed and the Order is no longer in the best

     interests of the child(ren) because: _____

     _____

     _____

     _____

FOR THESE REASONS, I request the Court change custody and/or visitation as follows: _____

_____
                    State the change that you are requesting

_____

_____ and order any other appropriate relief.

I solemnly affirm under the penalties of perjury that the contents of the foregoing paper are true to
the best of my knowledge, information, and belief.

_____   _____
         Date   Name   Dom.Rel. 7 (2 96)

Circuit Court for _____ Case No. _____
City or County

Name		Name	

Street Address _____ Apt. # VS. Street Address _____ Apt. #
( ) ( )
City State Zip Code Area Telephone City State Zip Code Area Telephone
Code Code
Plaintiff *Defendant*

COMPLAINT FOR ABSOLUTE DIVORCE
(Dom.Rel. 20)

I, _____ , representing myself, state that:
My name

1. The Defendant and I were married on _____
   Month   Day   Year

   in _____in a civil/religious ceremony.
   City/County/State where Married   Circle One

2. Check all that apply:

   ☐ I have lived in Maryland since: _____
   Month\Year

   ☐ My spouse has lived in Maryland since: _____
   Month\Year

   ☐ The grounds for divorce occurred in the State of Maryland.

3. ☐ We have no children together (skip paragraphs 4 and 5) or

   ☐ My spouse and I are the parents of the following child(ren):

Name	Date of Birth	Name	Date of Birth
Name	Date of Birth	Name	Date of Birth
Name	Date of Birth	Name	Date of Birth

4. The child(ren) are currently living with _____
   Name

5. It is in the best interest of the child(ren) that I have ☐ custody of   ☐ joint custody of

   ☐ visitation with : _____
   Name Child(ren)

6. I am/am not seeking alimony because_____
   Circle One

7. (You do not have to complete paragraph 7 if you are not asking the court to make decisions

   about your property.) My spouse and/or I have the following property and debts (check all

   that apply):

   ☐ House(s)   ☐ Furniture

   ☐ Pension(s)   ☐ Bank account(s) and investment(s)

   ☐ Motor Vehicle(s)   ☐ Other: _____

   ☐ Debts (attach list)

8. My grounds for an absolute divorce are: (Check all that apply)

☐ **Two-Year Separation** - From on or about _____, my spouse and I have lived
Month/Day/Year
separate and apart from each other in separate residences, without interruption, without sexual
intercourse, for more than two years and there is no reasonable expectation that we will
reconcile.

☐ **Voluntary Separation** - From on or about _____, my spouse and I by mutual
Month/Day/Year
and voluntary agreement have lived separate and apart from one another in separate residences,
without interruption, without sexual intercourse, for more than 12 months with the express
purpose and intent of ending our marriage, and there is no reasonable expectation that we will
reconcile.

☐ **Adultery** - My spouse committed adultery.

☐ **Actual Desertion** - On or about _____, my spouse, without just cause or
Month/Day/Year
reason, abandoned and deserted me, with the intention of ending our marriage. This
abandonment has continued without interruption for more than 12 months and there is no
reasonable expectation that we will reconcile.

☐ **Constructive Desertion** - I left my spouse because his/her cruel and vicious conduct made the
continuation of our marriage impossible, if I were to preserve my health, safety, and
self-respect. This conduct was the final and deliberate act of my spouse and our separation has
continued without interruption for more than 12 months and there is no reasonable expectation
that we will reconcile.

☐ **Criminal Conviction of a Felony or Misdemeanor** - On or about _____ , my
Month/Day/Year
spouse was sentenced to serve at least three years or an indeterminate sentence in a penal
institution and has served 12 or more months of the sentence.

☐ **Insanity** - On or about _____, my spouse was confined to a mental institution,
Month/Day/Year
hospital, or other similar institution and has been confined for 3 or more years. Two doctors
competent in psychiatry will testify that the insanity is incurable and there is no hope of
recovery. My spouse or I have been a resident of Maryland for at least two years before the
filing of this complaint.

FOR THESE REASONS, I request (check all that apply):

☑ An Absolute Divorce.
☐ A change back to my former name.

_____
Full Former Name
☐ Custody of the minor child(ren).
☐ Joint custody of the minor child(ren).
☐ Visitation with the minor child(ren).
☐ Use and possession of the family home and
family use personal property for a period of not
more than three years from the date of the divorce.

☐ Child support (Attach Form Dom.Rel.30
or Dom.Rel. 31).
☐ Health insurance for the child(ren).
☐ Health insurance for me.
☐ My share of the property or its value.
☐ A money award based on marital property.
☐ Alimony (Attach Form Dom.Rel.31).
☑ Any other appropriate relief.

_____   _____
Date   Name

Circuit Court for _____ Case No. _____
City or County

Name _____		Name _____
Street Address _____ Apt. #	VS.	Street Address _____ Apt. #
( )		( )
City State Zip Code Area Telephone		City State Zip Code Area Telephone
Code		Code
Plaintiff		*Defendant*

COMPLAINT FOR LIMITED DIVORCE
(Dom.Rel. 21)

I, _____ , representing myself, state that:
My name

1. The Defendant and I were married on _____
   Month   Day   Year

   in _____ in a civil/religious ceremony.
   City/County/State where Married   Circle One

2. Check all that apply:

   ☐   I have lived in Maryland since: _____
       Month\Year

   ☐   My spouse has lived in Maryland since: _____
       Month\Year

   ☐   The grounds for divorce occurred in the State of Maryland.

3. ☐   We have no children together (skip paragraphs 4 and 5) or

   ☐   My spouse and I are the parents of the following child(ren):

Name	Date of Birth	Name	Date of Birth
Name	Date of Birth	Name	Date of Birth
Name	Date of Birth	Name	Date of Birth

4. The child(ren) are currently living with _____
   Name

5. It is in the best interest of the child(ren) that I have ☐ custody of   ☐ joint custody of

   ☐ visitation with : _____
   Name Child(ren)

6. I am/am not seeking alimony because_____
   Circle One

7. (You do not have to complete paragraph 7 if you are not asking the court to make decisions

   about your property.) My spouse and/or I have the following property (check all that

   apply):

   ☐   Motor Vehicle(s)   ☐   Bank account(s) and investment(s)

   ☐   Furniture   ☐   Other: _____

8. My grounds for a limited divorce are: (Check all that apply)

☐ **Cruelty/Excessively Vicious Conduct Against Me** - My spouse has persistently treated me cruelly and has engaged in excessively vicious conduct rendering continuation of the marital relationship impossible if I am to preserve my health, safety, and self-respect.

☐ **Cruelty/Excessively Vicious Conduct Against My Children** - My spouse has persistently treated my minor child(ren) cruelly and has engaged in excessively vicious conduct against them rendering continuation of the marital relationship impossible if I am to preserve my minor child(ren)'s health, safety, and self-respect.

☐ **Actual Desertion** - On or about _____, my spouse, without just cause or
Month/Day/Year
reason, abandoned and deserted me, with the intention of ending our marriage. This abandonment has continued without interruption up to and including the time of filing of this complaint.

☐ **Constructive Desertion** - I left my spouse because his/her cruel and vicious conduct made the continuation of our marriage impossible, if I were to preserve my health, safety, and self-respect. This conduct was the final and deliberate act of my spouse and our separation has continued without interruption up to and including the time of the filing of this complaint.

☐ **Voluntary Separation** - From on or about_____, my spouse and I by mutual
Month/Day/Year
and voluntary agreement have lived separate and apart from one another in separate residences, without interruption, without sexual intercourse, with the express purpose and intent of ending our marriage, and there is no reasonable expectation that we will reconcile.

FOR THESE REASONS, I request (check all that apply):

☑ A Limited Divorce.
☐ Custody of the minor child(ren).
☐ Joint custody of the minor child(ren).
☐ Visitation with the minor child(ren).
☐ Child support (attach Form Dom.Rel. 30 or Dom.Rel. 31).
☐ Health insurance for the child(ren).
☐ Health insurance for me.
☐ Use and possession of the family home and family use personal property for a period of not more than three years from the date of the limited divorce.
☐ Alimony (attach Form Dom.Rel. 31).
☐ Resolution of personal property issues.
☑ Any other appropriate relief.

_____   _____
Date   Name

Circuit Court for _____ Case No. _____
City or County

Name _____ | Name _____

Street Address _____ Apt. # | VS. | Street Address _____ Apt. #

City   State   Zip Code   Area   Telephone | City   State   Zip Code   Area   Telephone
Code | Code
Plaintiff | **Defendant**

FINANCIAL STATEMENT
(Child Support)
(Dom.Rel. 30)

I, _____ , state that:
My name

I am the mother/father or _____
Circle One   State Relationship (for example, aunt, grandfather, guardian, etc.)

of the minor child(ren):

_____ _____ _____ _____
Name   Date of Birth   Name   Date of Birth

_____ _____ _____ _____
Name   Date of Birth   Name   Date of Birth

_____ _____ _____ _____
Name   Date of Birth   Name   Date of Birth

The following is a list of my income and expenses (see below*):

See definitions on back before filling out.

Total monthly income (before taxes) $ _____

Child support I am paying for my other child(ren) each month   _____

Monthly health insurance premium for this child(ren)   _____

Alimony I am paying each month to _____   _____
Name of Person(s)

Alimony I am receiving each month from _____   _____
Name of Person(s)

Work-related monthly child care expenses for this child(ren)   _____

Extraordinary monthly medical expenses for this child(ren)   _____

School and transportation expenses for this child(ren)   _____

To figure the monthly amount of expenses, weekly expenses should be multiplied by 4.3 and yearly expenses should be divided by 12. If you do not pay the same amount each month for any of the categories listed, figure what your average monthly expense is.

I solemnly affirm under the penalties of perjury that the contents of the foregoing paper are true to the best of my knowledge, information, and belief.

_____   _____
Date   Name

Total Monthly Income: Include income from all sources including self-employment, rent, royalties, business income, salaries, wages, commissions, bonuses, dividends, pensions, interest, trusts, annuities, social security benefits, workers compensation, unemployment benefits, disability benefits, alimony or maintenance received, tips, income from side jobs, severance pay, capital gains, gifts, prizes, lottery winnings, etc. Do not report benefits from means-tested public assistance programs such as food stamps or AFDC.

Extraordinary Medical Expenses: Uninsured expenses over $100 for a single illness or condition including orthodontia, dental treatment, asthma treatment, physical therapy, treatment for any chronic health problems, and professional counseling or psychiatric therapy for diagnosed mental disorders.

Child Care Expenses: Actual child care expenses incurred on behalf of a child due to employment or job search of either parent with amount to be determined by actual experience or the level required to provide quality care from a licensed source.

School and Transportation Expenses: Any expenses for attending a special or private elementary or secondary school to meet the particular needs of the child or expenses for transportation of the child between the homes of the parents.

Circuit Court for _____ Case No. _____
City or County

Name		Name	
Street Address	Apt. #	Street Address	Apt. #
	VS.		
City State Zip Code Area Code Telephone		City State Zip Code Area Code Telephone	
Plaintiff		**Defendant**	

FINANCIAL STATEMENT
(Alimony or Child Support)
(Dom.Rel. 31)

The following is a list of my income, expenses, assets, and liabilities:

MONTHLY INCOME *(See page 2)*		MONTHLY EXPENSES *(See below*)*	Myself	Children	Expenses Now Paid by Opposing Party
Gross income from employment	$_____	Rent or house payment	$_____	$_____	$_____
Less deductions:		Utilities: heat, gas, & electric			
Federal tax	_____	Telephone			
State tax	_____	Food			
FICA/Medicare	_____	Clothing			
Retirement	_____	Medical/dental *(Uninsured costs)*			
All other deductions: *(List & describe)*		Transportation			
_____	_____	Insurance: Life			
_____	_____	Health			
Net income from employment:	$_____	Auto			
Interest and other income from property and investments	_____	Other			
Income from all other sources: *(List & describe)*		Child care expense:			
		Work related			
_____	_____	Other			
_____	_____	Recreation			
Total Monthly Income:	$_____	Incidentals			
Additional monies received:		Periodic Pymts *(Attach list):*			
Tax refund *(divide annual refund by 12)*	_____	**Total Monthly Expenses:**	$_____	$_____	$_____
Monies from opposing party	_____				
Total Monthly Income and Monies Received	$_____				

ASSETS (What I own either by myself or with someone else):

	$
_____	_____
_____	_____
_____	_____
_____	_____
TOTAL ASSETS:	$_____

LIABILITIES (What I owe):

	$
_____	_____
_____	_____
_____	_____
_____	_____
TOTAL LIABILITIES:	$_____

Expenses should include expenses for children if they are residing with you. To figure the monthly amount of expenses, weekly expenses should be multiplied by 4.3 and yearly expenses should be divided by 12. If you do not pay the same amount each month for any of the categories listed, figure what your average monthly expense is.

I solemnly affirm under the penalties of perjury that the contents of the foregoing paper are true to the best of my knowledge, information, and belief.

_____   _____
Date   Name

Income: Include income from all sources including self-employment, rent, royalties, business income, salaries, wages, commissions, bonuses, dividends, pensions, interest, trusts, annuities, social security benefits, workers compensation, unemployment benefits, disability benefits, alimony or maintenance received, tips, income from side jobs, severance pay, capital gains, gifts, prizes, lottery winnings, etc. Do not report benefits from means-tested public assistance programs such as food stamps or AFDC.

Circuit Court for _____ Case No. _____
                           City or County

Name		Name

_____   VS.   _____

Street Address _____ Apt. #   Street Address _____ Apt. #

( )   ( )
City ____ State ___ Zip Code ___ Area ___ Telephone   City ____ State ___ Zip Code ___ Area ___ Telephone
                                 Code   Code
        Plaintiff   **Defendant**

MOTION FOR WAIVER OF PREPAYMENT OF FILING FEES
AND OTHER COURT COSTS
(Dom.Rel. 32)

I, _____ , representing myself, state that:
              My name

1.   I wish to file the form(s) entitled _____ ,
                                          Name(s) of Form(s)

     which I have completed and attached.

2.   I am currently unable to prepay filing fees and other court costs because of poverty.

3.   The answers to the following questions are true:

     (a)   Do you have any money? _____ How much? _____ Where? _____
     (b)   Are you employed? _____ Where? _____
           Position _____
     (c)   Are you self-employed? _____ Doing what? _____
     (d)   What is your rate of pay? _____
     (e)   Do you own an automobile? _____ Make _____ Year _____
           Is it paid for? _____ How much do you owe? _____ To whom? _____
           Where is the car? _____
     (f)   Do you owe any money to others? _____ How much? _____
           To whom? _____
     (g)   Do you own real estate? _____ Value? _____ Where? _____
     (h)   Do you own any other property of any kind? ____ What? _____
     (i)   Does anyone owe you money? ____ If so, state name, address and amount _____
           _____
     (j)   Do you receive money from any other source, including disability benefits,
           investments? _____ If, so how much? _____
     (k)   If married, give the name and address of your wife/husband _____
           _____
           Does your wife/husband work? _____ Where? _____
           _____ Rate of pay _____

4.   Other facts (if any) concerning my inability to prepay filing fees and other court costs are:
     _____
     _____
     _____

FOR THESE REASONS, I request waiver of prepayment of filing fees and other court costs and any other appropriate relief.

I solemnly affirm under the penalties of perjury that the contents of the foregoing paper are true to the best of my knowledge, information, and belief.

_____
Date

_____
Name

Circuit Court for _____ Case No. _____
City or County

_____
Name of Plaintiff

_____
Name of Defendant

ORDER
(Order to be completed by Court)

This Court grants the foregoing Motion.

_____
Judge

_____
Date

Circuit Court for _____ Case No. _____
                    City or County

<table>
<tr><td>Name</td><td rowspan="3">vs.</td><td>Name</td></tr>
<tr><td>Street Address   Apt. #
(   )</td><td>Street Address   Apt. #
(   )</td></tr>
<tr><td>City   State   Zip Code   Area   Telephone
                            Code
Plaintiff</td><td>City   State   Zip Code   Area   Telephone
                            Code
Defendant</td></tr>
</table>

JOINT STATEMENT OF PARTIES CONCERNING MARITAL AND NON-MARITAL PROPERTY
(Dom.Rel. 33)

1. The parties agree that the following property is "marital property" as defined by Code, Family Law Article, Section 8-201:

Description of Property	How Titled	Fair Market Value	Liens, Encumbrances, or Debt Directly Attributable

2. The parties agree that the following property is not marital property because the property (a) was acquired by one party before marriage, (b) was acquired by one party by inheritance or gift from a third person, (c) has been excluded by valid agreement, or (d) is directly traceable to any of these sources:

Description of Property	Reason Why Non-marital	How Titled	Fair Market Value	Liens, Encumbrances, or Debt Directly

3.   The parties are not in agreement as to whether the following property is marital or non-marital:

Description of Property	How Titled	Fair Market Value	Liens, Encumbrances, or Debt Directly Attributable

_____		_____
Date		Signature of Plaintiff or Attorney
_____		_____
Date		Signature of Defendant or Attorney

Instructions:

1.   If the parties do not agree concerning the title or value of any property, the parties shall set forth in the appropriate column a statement that the title or value is in dispute and each party's assertion relative to how the property is titled or the fair market value.

2.   In listing property that the parties agree is non-marital because the property is directly traceable to any of the listed sources of non-marital property, the parties shall specify the source to which the property is traceable.

Circuit Court for _____ Case No. _____
                        City or County

_____   _____
Name   Name

                                   VS.
_____ Apt. #   _____ Apt. #
Street Address   Street Address
                    (   )   (   )
_____   _____
City   State   Zip Code Area Telephone   City   State   Zip Code Area Telephone
                            Code   Code
            Plaintiff   *Defendant*

ANSWER TO ☐ COMPLAINT ☐ PETITION ☐ MOTION
                          (Dom.Rel. 50)

I, _____ representing myself, answering the

_____
          Name of Complaint, Petition, or Motion that you are answering

filed against me, state:

1. Answering Paragraph No. 1 (check one):
   ☐ I admit all of the statement(s) in Paragraph No. 1.
   ☐ I deny all of the statements(s) in Paragraph No. 1, except I admit that _____

   _____
                  (State the facts that you admit or write "none")
   ☐ I do not have enough information to know whether or not the statement(s) in Para. 1 are true.

2. Answering Paragraph No. 2 (check one):
   ☐ I admit all of the statement(s) in Paragraph No. 2.
   ☐ I deny all of the statements(s) in Paragraph No. 2, except I admit that _____

   _____
                  (State the facts that you admit or write "none")
   ☐ I do not have enough information to know whether or not the statement(s) in Para. 2 are true.
   ☐ There is no Paragraph No. 2.

3. Answering Paragraph No. 3 (check one):
   ☐ I admit all of the statement(s) in Paragraph No. 3.
   ☐ I deny all of the statements(s) in Paragraph No. 3, except I admit that _____

   _____
                  (State the facts that you admit or write "none")
   ☐ I do not have enough information to know whether or not the statement(s) in Para. 3 are true.
   ☐ There is no Paragraph No. 3.

4. Answering Paragraph No. 4 (check one):
   ☐ I admit all of the statement(s) in Paragraph No. 4.
   ☐ I deny all of the statements(s) in Paragraph No. 4, except I admit that _____

   _____
                  (State the facts that you admit or write "none")
   ☐ I do not have enough information to know whether or not the statement(s) in Para. 4 are true.
   ☐ There is no Paragraph No. 4.

5. Answering Paragraph No. 5 (check one):
   ☐ I admit all of the statement(s) in Paragraph No. 5.
   ☐ I deny all of the statements(s) in Paragraph No. 5, except I admit that _____

   _____
                  (State the facts that you admit or write "none")
   ☐ I do not have enough information to know whether or not the statement(s) in Para. 5 are true.
   ☐ There is no Paragraph No. 5.

6. Answering Paragraph No. 6 (check one):

☐ I admit all of the statement(s) in Paragraph No. 6.

☐ I deny all of the statements(s) in Paragraph No. 6, except I admit that _____

_____
(State the facts that you admit or write "none")

☐ I do not have enough information to know whether or not the statement(s) in Para. 6 are true.

☐ There is no Paragraph No. 6.

7. Answering Paragraph No. 7 (check one):

☐ I admit all of the statement(s) in Paragraph No. 7.

☐ I deny all of the statements(s) in Paragraph No. 7, except I admit that _____

_____
(State the facts that you admit or write "none")

☐ I do not have enough information to know whether or not the statement(s) in Para. 7 are true.

☐ There is no Paragraph No. 7.

8. Answering Paragraph No. 8 (check one):

☐ I admit all of the statement(s) in Paragraph No. 8.

☐ I deny all of the statements(s) in Paragraph No. 8, except I admit that _____

_____
(State the facts that you admit or write "none")

☐ I do not have enough information to know whether or not the statement(s) in Para. 8 are true.

☐ There is no Paragraph No. 8.

9. In my defense, I also want the Court to consider the following facts (A copy of any court Order relating to my defense is attached, if available): _____

_____

_____

FOR THESE REASONS, I request the Court (check all that apply):

☐ Dismiss/deny the Complaint/Petition/Motion.

☐ Grant the relief requested in the Complaint/Petition/Motion.

☐ Grant the relief requested in the Complaint/Petition/Motion, except _____

_____
(State the relief you do not want the Court to grant)

☑ Order any other appropriate relief.

_____   _____

Date   Name

CERTIFICATE OF SERVICE

I HEREBY CERTIFY that on this _____ day of _____, 19____ , a copy of the foregoing Answer was mailed, postage prepaid, to _____

Opposing Party or His/Her Attorney

_____

Opposing Party's or His/Her Attorney's Address including City/State/Zip

_____   _____

Date   Your Signature

IMPORTANT (TIME FOR FILING YOUR ANSWER IF YOU WISH TO CONTEST THIS MATTER): You must file your Answer with the Court within the time stated in the Summons. If you were served with a "Motion" but no summons, you must file your Answer within 15 days after being served.

IMPORTANT (ADDITIONAL PAPERS YOU MUST FILE): If the Opposing Party is seeking child support, alimony, or both, you must complete and attach to your Answer the appropriate financial statement(s) (child support - use Form Dom.Rel.30 or Dom.Rel.31; alimony - use Form Dom.Rel.31). If you want the Court to grant relief to you, you must complete page 3 of this form and file the appropriate additional form(s).

Instructions: If you want something *different* from what the other side wants, check below and fill out the appropriate Dom.Rel. Form(s). See General Instructions and Forms Dom.Rel. 1 through 21.

COUNTERCLAIM

I, _____ representing myself, state that:

1. I want (check all that apply):

   ☐ child support

   ☐ custody

   ☐ visitation

   ☐ modification of child support

   ☐ modification of custody/visitation

   ☐ absolute divorce

   ☐ limited divorce

2. I have attached Form(s) Dom.Rel. _____

   _____
   (List form numbers of the DOMREL forms you completed)

   to this Answer and I request that the Form(s) I have attached be considered as my

   counterclaim against the other side.

_____   _____
            Date   Name

CERTIFICATE OF SERVICE

I HEREBY CERTIFY that on this _____ day of _____ , 19_____ ,
a copy of this Counterclaim and a copy of the forms listed in Paragraph 2, above, were mailed,
postage prepaid, to

_____
Opposing Party or His/Her Attorney

_____
Opposing Party's or His/Her Attorney's Address including City/State/Zip

_____   _____
            Date   Signature

Circuit Court for _____ Case No. _____
                        City or County

_____		_____
Name		Name
_____ Apt. #	VS.	_____ Apt. #
Street Address		Street Address
( )		( )
_____		_____
City State Zip Code Area Telephone		City State Zip Code Area Telephone
Code		Code
Plaintiff		*Defendant*

REQUEST FOR MASTER'S HEARING
(Dom.Rel. 51)

Please schedule, at the Court's earliest convenience, the above-captioned matter for a hearing

before a Master on the issues of (check all that apply):

- ☐ custody.

- ☐ visitation.

- ☐ child support.

- ☐ alimony.

- ☐ use and possession of the family home and/or family use personal property.

_____   _____
            Date   Signature

CERTIFICATE OF SERVICE

I HEREBY CERTIFY that on this_____ day of _____, 19____ , a copy of this

Request for Master's Hearing was mailed, postage prepaid, to _____
                                                              Opposing Party or His/Her Attorney

                                                    _____
                                                              Address

                                                    _____
                                                              City/State/Zip

_____   _____
            Date   Signature

Circuit Court for _____ Case No. _____
City or County

_____	_____
Name	Name

VS.

_____   _____
Street Address   Apt. #   Street Address   Apt. #

( )   ( )
_____   _____
City   State   Zip Code   Area   Telephone   City   State   Zip Code   Area   Telephone
                                 Code   Code
Plaintiff   **Defendant**

REQUEST FOR TRIAL ON THE MERITS
(Dom.Rel. 52)

Please schedule the above-captioned case for a trial on the merits at the Court's earliest

convenience.

_____   _____
Date   Signature

CERTIFICATE OF SERVICE

I HEREBY CERTIFY that on this_____ day of _____, 19____ , a copy of this

Request for trial on the merits was mailed, postage prepaid, to _____
                                                                Opposing Party or His/Her Attorney

                                                                _____
                                                                Address

                                                                _____
                                                                City/State/Zip

_____   _____
Date   Signature

Circuit Court for _____ Case No._____

City or County

_____   _____

Name   **vs.**   **Name**
  Plaintiff   **Defendant**

SHOW CAUSE ORDER
(Form to be Completed by Court)
(Dom.Rel.53)

UPON consideration of the Petition for Contempt and the facts asserted in the Petition, which are

incorporated by reference herein, this Court ORDERS the Plaintiff/Defendant, _____

_____, to appear in person, in this Court, located at_____

_____in Room_____on the _____day of _____,

at_____a.m/p.m. and to show cause, if any, why the Plaintiff/Defendant should not be granted the relief

requested in the Complaint for Contempt, provided that a copy of the Complaint for Contempt and this

Order shall be served on the Plaintiff/Defendant or his/her attorney of record, by _____

_____on or before the_____day of _____

_____,199__. Any written answer shall be filed by the Plaintiff/Defendant on or before the _____

day of _____,19____ .

_____
Judge

_____
Date

If jail time is requested in the Petition, read the notice on the back of this Show Cause Order.

Serve on:_____

_____
Address

_____

_____

Method of Service_____

Notice to Person Whose Jail Time Is Requested

TO THE PERSON ALLEGED TO BE IN CONTEMPT OF COURT:

1. It is alleged that you have disobeyed a court order, are in contempt of court, and should go to jail until you obey the court's order.
2. You have the right to have a lawyer. If you already have a lawyer, you should consult the lawyer at once. If you do not have a lawyer, please note:

    (a) A lawyer can be helpful to you by:

    (1) explaining the allegations against you;

    (2) helping you determine and present any defense to those allegations;

    (3) explaining to you the possible outcomes; and

    (4) helping you at the hearing.

    (b) Even if you do not plan to content that you are in contempt of court, a lawyer can be helpful.

    (c) If you want a lawyer but do not have the money to hire one, the Public Defender may provide a lawyer for you. You must contact the Public Defender at least 10 business days before the date of the hearing. The court clerk will tell you how to contact the Public Defender.

    (d) If you want a lawyer but you cannot get one and the Public Defender will not provide one for you, contact the court clerk as soon as possible.

    (e) DO NOT WAIT UNTIL THE DATE OF YOUR HEARING TO GET A LAWYER. If you do not have a lawyer before the hearing date, the court may find that you have waived your right to a lawyer, and the hearing may be held with you unrepresented by a lawyer.

    (3) IF YOU DO NOT APPEAR FOR THE HEARING, YOU MAY BE SUBJECT TO ARREST.

Circuit Court for _____ Case No. _____
                          City or County

Name		Name
Street Address Apt. #	VS.	Street Address Apt. #
( )		( )
City State Zip Code Area Telephone		City State Zip Code Area Telephone
Code		Code
Plaintiff		*Defendant*

REQUEST FOR ORDER OF DEFAULT
(Dom.Rel. 54)

I, _____ , representing myself, request an Order of Default
                My Name

against _____ for failure to plead as provided by the Maryland
                Opposing Party

Rules. The last known address of the opposing party is _____

_____

_____

_____   _____
            Date   Name

NON-MILITARY AFFIDAVIT

_____ :
        Opposing Party

1.   is not in the military service of the United States;

2.   is not in the military service of any nation allied with the United States;

3.   has not been ordered to report for induction under the Selective Training and Service Act;
      and

4.   is not a member of the Enlisted Reserve Corps who has been ordered to report for military
      service.

I solemnly affirm under the penalties of perjury that the contents of the foregoing paper are true to
the best of my knowledge, information, and belief.

_____   _____
            Date   Name

Circuit Court for _____ Case No. _____
City or County

_____   _____
Name of Plaintiff   Name of Defendant

ORDER OF DEFAULT
(Order to be Completed by Court)

This Court enters an Order of Default against _____ for
Opposing Party

failure to plead, and orders that testimony to support the allegations of the Complaint be taken

before ☐ one of the Judges or ☐ a Standing Examiner/Master of this Court.

_____
Judge

_____
Date

IMPORTANT: Person obtaining Order of Default must contact the Clerk's Office at

_____ for further instructions to schedule a hearing.
Telephone Number

Circuit Court for _____ Case No. _____
City or County

_____   _____
Name   Name

_____   _____
Street Address   Apt. # VS. Street Address   Apt. #
              ( )   ( )
_____   _____
City   State   Zip Code Area Telephone City   State   Zip Code Area Telephone
                             Code   Code
              Plaintiff   Defendant

AFFIDAVIT OF SERVICE
(Private Process)
(Dom.Rel. 55)

I certify that I served_____ at _____ a.m./p.m.
                        Name of person served   Time   Circle One

on _____, 19____, at _____,
       Date   Street Address   City   State   Zip Code

by delivering and leaving with _____
                                       Name of person served

a copy of the _____
                      Name of ALL pleadings/documents served

which were previously filed with this Court. Attached is a copy of any summons ("process")

issued by the Court, the original of which I served upon the person served. I certify that I am over

eighteen (18) years of age and I am not the Plaintiff or the Defendant.

I SOLEMNLY AFFIRM under the penalties of perjury that the contents of the foregoing paper are
true to the best of my knowledge, information, and belief.

_____   _____
Date   Name of Server (signature)

                                 _____
                                 Name of Server (printed or typed)

                                 _____
                                 Street Address   City   State   Zip Code of Server
                                 ( )
                                 _____
                                 Area Code   Telephone Number of Server

Circuit Court for _____ Case No. _____
City or County

_____		_____
Name		Name
_____ Apt. #	VS.	_____ Apt. #
Street Address		Street Address
( )		( )
_____ Area Telephone		_____ Area Telephone
City State Zip Code Code		City State Zip Code Code
Plaintiff		**Defendant**

AFFIDAVIT OF SERVICE
(Certified Mail)
(Dom.Rel. 56)

I certify that I served a copy of the_____
Name of ALL pleadings/documents served

(which were previously filed with this Court) upon _____
Name of person served

on _____ , 19____ , at _____
Date   Street Address   City   State   Zip Code

by certified mail, restricted delivery, return receipt requested. The **original** return receipt signed

by _____ is attached. Also attached is a copy of any
Name of person served

summons ("process") issued by the Court, the original of which I included in the certified mail

service upon the person served. I certify that I am over eighteen (18) years of age and I am not the

Plaintiff or the Defendant.

I SOLEMNLY AFFIRM under the penalties of perjury that the contents of the foregoing paper are
true to the best of my knowledge, information, and belief.

_____   _____
Date   Name of person certifying service (signature)

                                              _____
                                              Name of person certifying service (printed or typed)

                                              _____
                                              Street Address   City   State   Zip Code
                                              of person certifying service
                                              ( )
                                              _____
                                              Area Code   Telephone Number of person certifying service

Dom.Rel. 56 (2 96)

Circuit Court for _____ Case No. _____
                        City or County

_____ VS. _____
Name   Name

       Plaintiff   *Defendant*

ORDER
(Dom.Rel. 57)

UPON consideration of the papers and pleadings filed in this case, it is this _____

day of _____ , 19 _____, by this Court, ORDERED:

_____

_____

_____

_____

_____

_____

_____

_____

_____

_____

_____

_____

                              _____
                                           Judge

```
                                   *
                                   *  IN THE CIRCUIT COURT
                                   *
                                   *        FOR
                                   *
            PLAINTIFF             *
                                   *        COUNTY
        VS.                        *
                                   *
                                   *
                                   *  CASE NUMBER:
                                   *
            DEFENDANT             *
****************************************************************
```

EARNINGS WITHHOLDING ORDER

TO EMPLOYER: _____
             _____
             _____
             _____
             _____

        Pursuant to Maryland Code Ann. Family Law Article Sub-section 10-120 through 10-134, it is by the Circuit Court for Carroll County this _____ day of _____,19_____, ORDERED, That

        (1) You are required by Maryland Law to withhold and forward support payments from the earnings of:

Name: _____   Soc. Sec. No.:_____

        (2) You must begin to withhold the support at the <u>beginning of the next pay period</u> on a regular and continuing basis in accordance with the following schedule and subject to the following limitations and conditions, and subject to further Court Order:

        (a) <u>Schedule for Current Support:</u>

The current support order provides for $_____ per _____ for child support and $_____ per_____ for spousal support or $_____ per _____ for non-differentiated support. If you pay:

Weekly: Deduct $_____per pay
Biweekly: Deduct $_____per pay
Semimonthly: Deduct $_____per pay
Monthly: Deduct $_____per pay

        (B) <u>Schedule for Arrears:</u>

In addition to the amount deducted under this Order for current support, you must make deductions for arrears of $_____ in child support and $_____ in spousal support of $_____ for non-differentiated support. If you pay:

```
Weekly:          Deduct $_____per pay
Biweekly:        Deduct $_____per pay
Semimonthly:     Deduct $_____per pay
Monthly:         Deduct $_____per pay
```

Discontinue these deductions for arrears when you have deducted, <u>under this schedule</u>, a total of $_____, in addition to any other accumulated arrearage. DO NOT, however, discontinue any deduction under the schedule for current support unless the Court so orders or, under paragraph (1) of this Order, you are unable to deliver the payments.

(c) <u>Limitations on Deduction:</u>

You may not deduct more from your employee's earnings than permitted by the Federal Consumer Protection Act (15 U. S. C., Sub-section 1673 (b)). For employees who are supporting second families, the maximum you can withhold is 50% of net income. For other employees, the maximum is 60%. If you are deducting overdue support (see above), those maximums are increased to 55% and 65% respectively.

(d) <u>Remittance:</u>

You are required to forward amounts withheld from the earnings of an employee to _____
within ten (10) days of the day on which the earnings are paid to the employee. You shall send all deductions required under this Order to:

_____

_____

_____

CASE NUMBER:
and Employees name,

_____
<u>must be written on ALL checks and correspondence.</u>

(e) <u>Optional Deduction:</u>

To help offset your expenses, you may deduct and keep an extra $2.00 during each pay period in which you make a deduction under this Order.

(f) <u>Non-Discrimination:</u>

You may not use withholding as a basis for reprisal, dismissal, or refusal to hire or promote any employee.

(g) <u>Penalties:</u>

<u>If you wilfully fail to withhold and forward the deducted payments as required by the Order, you are liable for the amount you fail to deduct and are subject to civil penalties.</u>

(h) Change of Employment:

You must notify the Court within __ten (10) days__ after you learn that the employee is leaving your employ and include, if available, a social security number, home address, and new place of employment.

(i) Inability to Deliver:

If you are unable to deliver payments for __two__ consecutive months, because the recipient failed to notify you of an address change, stop making deductions, return the undeliverable payments to the employee and notify the Court.

_____
Judge (Signature)

INSTRUCTION FOR EARNINGS WITHHOLDING

If for some reason an employee is not paid, continue to make the regular deduction on the next pay day. Do not attempt to double payments.

If the full amount required to be deducted by the Order cannot be deducted because the employee's pay is inadequate, enclose with your remittance an explanation of how you calculated the amount of deduction.

Include the employee's name and Social Security number on your remittance (or case number).

Payments that you deduct for several employees which are to be mailed to the same recipient or agency may be sent in one check so long as you identify the amount withheld for each employee.

Support withholding orders are similar to commercial liens but take priority over any other lien under State law. You must withhold the support order first.

    Total deductions for arrears under schedule (b) made to date are $_____.

Notice of Change in Employment

Send to: Case No.:

Obligor's Name:_____
Soc. Sec. No.:_____

Obligor's Home Address:_____

Effective_____, 19_____, Obligor will leave (left) my Employ.

New Employer:_____

                                       _____
                                       Current or Former Employer

                                       _____
                                       Name

                                       _____
                                       Address

                                       _____
                                       Phone Number

Help Beyond This Book

Although this book covers all of the major domestic relations actions in some detail, it doesn't come close to covering everything. That would require a much more detailed treatise, most of which would be irrelevant for nearly all readers. If you want to research in a more detailed treatise, a good starting point is *Maryland Family Law* by Hon. John F. Fader, II and Richard J. Gilbert, The Michie Company, 1996. It is the leading textbook on Maryland Family Law and the one that many law students in Maryland study from and which lawyers use on a day-to-day basis.

Another good source are the family law publications of MICPEL, The Maryland Institute for Continuing Professional Education for Lawyers, Inc., Suite 830 Candler Building, 111 Market Place, Baltimore, Maryland 21202-4012, Phone: (410) 659-6730 or (800)787-0068, and on the World Wide Web at: http://www.micpel.edu.

If you want to learn more about Maryland Civil Procedure, a good starting point is *Maryland Civil Procedure, Forms and Practice*, by Robert D. Klein and Edward S. Digges, Jr., Aspen Publications, 1995.

The Women's Law Center of Maryland, Inc., maintains a *pro se* telephone hotline that will provide answers to questions on the use of the Dom. Rel. forms. Phone: (410) 321-8761 for current hours.

There is a growing body of family law resources on the Internet. A good place to start is The People's Law Library of Maryland at http://www.peoples-law.com which contains copies of the Dom. Rel. forms. Another resource is the Divorce Law Information Service Center at http://www.divorcelawinfo.com, which offers marital separation agreement kits and divorce form kits that can be down-loaded and completed on-line for Maryland, Virginia, the District of Columbia, Pennsylvania, and Florida.

The author of this book also maintains a Web site that offers a fee-based legal advice and information service, known as the Maryland On-Line Family Law Advisor. It provides on-line Maryland family law information services. It is located at http://www.granat.com and E-mail: richard@granat.com.

For those who do not have access to the Internet, and want to purchase the Dom. Rel. forms together with a Maryland Separation Agreement Kit on floppy disk, they are available for a price of **$25.00,** plus **$3.00** shipping, plus 5% Maryland sales tax for a total of **$29.25** from:
> Network Legal Solutions, Inc.
> 5430 Lynx Lane, Suite 135
> Columbia, Maryland 21044
> 1-888-2-LEGAL-9, or (301)-596-8818
> Please indicate the word-processing format when ordering: Available in Word, Wordperfect, Word for Macintosh, and MS Works.